THE

PRIMARY STANDARD SPEAKER.

CONTAINING

ORIGINAL AND SELECTED PIECES,

ESPECIALLY ADAPTED TO

DECLAMATION.

FOR THE YOUNGEST PUPILS.

BY

EPES SARGENT,

AUTHOR OF THE "STANDARD SPEAKER," "THE INTERMEDIATE STANDARD SPEAKER," "THE STANDARD SERIES OF READERS," ETC.

WITH ILLUSTRATIONS.

PHILADELPHIA:
PUBLISHED BY CHARLES DESILVER.
1857.

PREFACE.

THE present work is the smallest of a series of three Speakers, of which the Standard Speaker is the first and largest, and the Intermediate Standard Speaker the second in size and importance.

The fault found with most compilations of this rank is, that the pieces proposed for declamation do not differ, in their level tone, from those in ordinary reading-books. I have endeavored to avoid this objection, and to present such exercises as are especially suited to be committed to memory and spoken by the young.

Many of these exercises, some without names of authors, and others with various names appended, are now for the first time published. They include several of the translations from French and German writers, and, being original, are protected by the copyright. While I have retained many favorite old pieces, which could not well be dispensed with, much that is wholly new will accordingly be found in the present volume.

ELECTROTYPED BY HOBART AND ROBBINS, BOSTON.

TABLE OF CONTENTS.

PROSE.

POETRY.

DIALOGUES.

SARGENT'S
PRIMARY
STANDARD SPEAKER.

THE STUDIOUS BOY.

SEE him at his book. He has a piece to declaim at school. Do you want to know what he is doing? He is looking out in the dictionary every doubtful word in his piece. He does not mean to make a blunder, if he can help it.

There are some common words, about the pronunciation of which he is almost sure, but not quite. He looks out the word *hearth,* for he heard a boy, the other day, pronounce it as if it rhymed with *earth.* But he finds that *ea* in *hearth* ought to have the sound it has in *heart.*

He looks out the words *heard, evil, even,* and *heaven.* What common words! But he has heard them mispronounced. He finds that the *ea* in *heard* has the sound of *e* in *her;* that the *i* in *evil*, and the *e* in the last syllables in *heaven* and *even*, are not sounded.

After he has learnt how to pronounce all the words in his piece, he will declaim it aloud by himself, till he can repeat it all without looking on the book. If there is any sentence which he does not understand in his piece, he will ask his mother or his teacher to explain it.

The studious boy can *play* as well as *study*. He does not pore over his book too long. He will go and play at ball, or take a walk with his sister, as soon as he has finished his lesson in pronunciation. The studious boy will be a good speaker, for he sets about his task in earnest, and takes the right means. If you would succeed in any thing, *be in earnest*.

A BOY'S SPEECH AGAINST SHOOTING BIRDS.

Boys, I have mounted this stump to speak my mind about shooting birds for sport. I know four or five fellows who go about with bows and arrows, and pistols, and shoot at robins, blackbirds, bobolinks, and sparrows, without caring for them when they are killed, but doing it merely to show that they can take good aim. Now, I 'm a small boy, but I don't care who hears me when I say that the practice is mean and cruel.

Any farmer will tell you that the birds do more good than harm. They destroy insects and vermin. A woodpecker will clear a tree of worms that would have lodged beneath the bark and sapped the life of the trunk. A robin, while he puts his bill into your best cherries, will do you service in keeping off rose-bugs and other enemies. I say nothing about the cheering songs and pleasant warbling of the birds. The boy who does not love to hear them has no music in his soul. But just think of the folly and cruelty of shooting them ; —

the folly, in killing the friends of your trees; the cruelty, in killing them wantonly, and at seasons when they have young ones to take care of!

Heaven has given us power over the poor dumb animals. We may kill them for food, — making them suffer as little as possible. But to kill any one for mere sport is a hateful practice. I love to see animals enjoying life. Especially I love to see and hear the birds. Never will I knowingly play with the boy who kills them for his amusement merely. Never will I blend my pleasure or my pride "with sorrow of the meanest thing that feels." CHARLES.

Study to articulate your words distinctly, and pronounce them aright. In the preceding piece do not slur the *t* in *insects;* give the *th* in *beneath* its vocal sound, as in *breathe;* give the *o* in *nothing* the sound of short *u*, as in *hut;* give the *ing* its full sound, as in *king;* give the *ow* in *fellow*, *arrow*, *sorrow*, &c., the sound of long *o;* do not say *feller*, &c.

SMALL SERVICE IS TRUE SERVICE.

WHAT if a drop of rain should plead,
"So small a drop as I
Can ne'er refresh the thirsty mead:
I'll tarry in the sky!"

What if the shining beam of noon
Should in its fountain stay,
Because its feeble light alone
Can not create a day!

Does not each rain-drop help to form
The cool, refreshing shower?
And every ray of light to warm
And beautify the flower?

FORGET YOUR INJURIES.

UNWISE and unhappy is he who can not forgive and forgĕt his injuries. The remembrance of them will come like a dark shadow across his heart, and embitter every fount of happiness. The de′mon of hate will reign in his bosom, and make him, of all accountable creatures, the most miserable.

Have you been injured in purse or in character? Let the smiling angel of forgiveness drive every resentful feeling from your soul, and shed its sunshine around your thoughts. Study not how you may revenge yourself, but study how you may return good for evil.

There was once a good bishop, named Boulter, whose constant habit it was to forgive all those who injured him; and the consequence was that he always enjoyed peace of mind. The following lines were written on him after his death. Who would not desire such an epitaph?

"Some write their wrongs in marble; — he, more just,
Stooped down serene, and wrote them in the dust;
There trod them down, the sport of every wind,
Swept from the earth, and blotted from his mind:
There, buried and effaced, he bade them lie,
And grieved they could not 'scape the Almighty's eye."

THE CONTENTED BLIND BOY.

O! SAY, what is that thing called light,
Which I must ne'er enjoy?
What are the blessings of the sight?
O! tell a poor blind boy!

You talk of wondrous things you *see;*
You say the sun shines bright;
I feel him warm, but how can he
Or make it day or night?

My day or night myself I make
Whene'er I sleep or play;
And could I always keep awake,
With me 't were always day.

With heavy sighs I often hear
You mourn my hapless woe;
But sure with patience I can bear
A loss I ne'er can know.

Then let not what I can not have
My cheer of mind destroy;
While thus I sing, I am a king,
Although a poor blind boy.

CIBBER.

THE SEASONS.

Spring.

Who is this beautiful virgin that approaches, clothed in a robe of light green? She has a garland of flowers on her head, and flowers spring up wherever she sets her foot. The snow which covered the fields, and the ice which was in the rivers, melt away when she breathes upon them. The young lambs frisk about her, and the birds warble in their little throats, to welcome her coming; and when they see her, they begin to choose their mates, and to build their nests. Youths and maidens, have you seen this beautiful virgin? If you have, tell me who is she, and what is her name.

Summer.

Who is this that comes from the south, thinly clad in a light, transparent garment? Her breath is hot and sultry; she seeks the refreshment of the cool shade; she seeks the clear streams, the crystal brooks, to bathe her languid limbs. The brooks and rivulets fly from her, and are dried up at her approach. She cools her parched lip with berries, and the grateful acid of fruits, the seedy melon, the sharp apple, and the red pulp of the juicy cherry, which are poured out plentifully around her. The tanned hay-makers welcome her coming; and the sheep-shearer, who clips the fleeces of his flock with his sounding shears. When she comes, let me lie under the thick shade of a spreading beech-tree; let me walk with her in the early morning, when the dew is yet upon the grass; let me wander with her in the soft twilight, when the shepherd shuts his fold, and the star of evening appears. Youths and maidens, tell me, if you know, who is she, and what is her name.

Autumn.

Who is he that comes with sober pace, stealing upon us unawares? His garments are red with the blood of the grape, and his temples are bound with a sheaf of ripe wheat. His hair is thin and begins to fall, and the auburn is mixed with mournful gray. He shakes the brown nuts from the tree. He winds the horn, and calls the hunters to their sports. The gun sounds. The trembling partridge and the beautiful pheasant flutter, bleeding, in the air, and fall dead at the sportsman's feet. Who is he that is crowned with the wheat-sheaf? Youths and maidens, tell me, if you know, who is he, and what is his name.

Winter.

Who is he that comes from the north, clothed in furs and warm wool? He wraps his cloak close about him. His head is bald; his beard is made of sharp icicles. He loves the blazing fire, high piled upon the hearth. He binds skates to his feet, and skims over the frozen lakes. His breath is piercing and cold, and no little flower peeps above the surface of the ground when he is by. Whatever he touches turns to ice. If he were to strike you with his cold hand, you would be quite stiff and dead, like a piece of marble. Youths and maidens, do you see him? He is coming fast upon us, and soon he will be here. Tell me, if you know, who is he, and what is his name. BARBAULD.

Give the *oa* in *throat* the sound of long *o;* the *ph* in *pheasant* the sound of *f;* the *ea* in *hearth* the sound of *a* in *father*. Sound the aspirate in *wheat*. The *ee* in *been* has the sound of short *i*, as in *pin;* the *ai* in *again*, *against*, has the sound of short *e*, as in *pen;* the *o* in *none* has the sound of short *u*, as in *gun*. In *get*, *yet*, *forget*, &c., give the *e* the sound it has in *pen*. Do not say *git*, *yit*, &c. The *t* and *e* in *often* are not sounded. Do not say *jest* instead of *just*, or *sence* instead of *since*.

TRUST NOT TO APPEARANCES.

Early one day in leafy June,
When brooks and birds are all in tune,
A Quaker, on a palfrey brown,
Was riding over Horsley Down.

Though he could see no houses near,
He trotted on without a fear;
For not a thief upon the road
Would guess where he his cash had stowed.

As thus he went — that Quaker sly —
Another Quaker trotted by: —
"Stop, brother," said the first; "the weather
Is pleasant — let us chat together."

"Nay," said the stranger, "know'st thou not
That this is a suspected spot?
That robbers here resort, my brother?" —
"A fig for robbers!" said the other:

"I 've all my money in a note,
And that is hid — not in my coat —
But —" — "Where?" the other asked. — "Behold!" —
"What! in your shoe?" — "The secret 's told!

"You see, it has a double sole:
Within that I have hid the whole:
Now, where 's the robber who would think
Of ever looking there for chink?" —

"Here!" cried the stranger; "so dismount,
And straightway render an account:
I 'm Captain Bibb, the robber trim;
So hand your money quick to him!

"Don't tremble — all you 've got to do,
You know, is to take off your shoe;
And for your money I will give
Advice shall serve you while you live.

"Don't take each broad-brim chance may send,
Though plain his collar, for a Friend ·
Don't trust in gentleman or clown
While riding over Horsley Down."

OSBORNE.

AMERICAN BOYS TO GENERAL HOWE.

At the time the British held possession of Boston, during the Revolution, a party of boys, who had been molested by the king's soldiers, went to the British commander, and made complaint, after the following manner:

"WE have come, General Howe, to make our complaints at head-quarters, against your soldiers. They persist in plaguing us at our sports; and we are resolved not to stand it any longer. If we raise a kite, some of your red-coats will come along and cut the string. If we play at ball, they will pick up the ball, and throw it where we can not find it. They have scattered our marbles. They have spoiled our coasting-grounds. They have cut up the ice on the Frog Pond, so that we might not slide and skate. In every way they try to molest and provoke us. We are American boys, General Howe, and we have a right to play on the Common, and your soldiers have no right to prevent us. We have heard that you are a just man; and we are here to ask you to put a stop at once to these practices on the part of your soldiers. We thank you for hearing us so attentively; we see by your friendly looks that our complaints will not pass unheeded. We shall clear another coasting-ground this afternoon, and we shall look to you, sir, to protect us in our rights, and forbid all annoyances from your soldiers. If you will not do this, General Howe, we must protect ourselves; for we are determined never to surrender the smallest of our rights — no, not to the king himself."

WHO STOLE THE BIRD'S NEST?

To whit! To whit! To whee!
Will you listen to me?
Who stole four eggs I laid,
And the nice nest I made?

Not I, said the cow, Moo-oo!
Such a thing I 'd never do.
I gave you a wisp of hay,
But did n't take your nest away.
Not I, said the cow, Moo-oo!
Such a thing I 'd never do.

To whit! To whit! To whee!
Will you listen to me?
Who stole four eggs I laid,
And the nice nest I made?

Bobolink! Bobolink!
Now, what do you think?
Who stole a nest away
From the plum-tree to-day?

Not I, said the dog, Bow-wow,
I would n't be so mean, I vow.
I gave hairs the nest to make,
But the nest I did not take.
Not I, said the dog, Bow-wow!
I would n't be so mean, I vow.

To whit! To whit! To whee!
Will you listen to me?
Who stole four eggs I laid,
And the nice nest I made?

Bobolink! Bobolink!
Now, what do you think?
Who stole a nest away
From the plum-tree to-day?

Coo-coo! Coo-coo! Coo-coo!
Let me speak a word, too.
Who stole that pretty nest,
From little yellow-breast?

Not I, said the sheep; O, no,
I would n't treat a poor bird so.

I gave wool the nest to line,
But the nest was none of mine.
Baa, baa! said the sheep; O, no,
I would n't treat a poor bird so.

To whit! To whit! To whee!
Will you listen to me?
Who stole four eggs I laid,
And the nice nest I made?

Bobolink! Bobolink!
Now, what do you think?
Who stole a nest away
From the plum-tree to-day?

Coo-coo! Coo-coo! Coo!
Let me speak a word, too.
Who stole that pretty nest
From little yellow-breast?

Caw! Caw! cried the crow,
I should like to know
What thief took away
A bird's nest to-day?

Cluck! cluck! said the hen,
Don't ask me again!
Why, I have n't a chick
Would do such a trick.

We all gave her a feather,
And she wove them together.
I 'd scorn to intrude
On her and her brood.

Cluck! cluck! said the hen,
Don't ask me again.

Chirr-a-whirr! Chirr-a-whirr!
We will make a great stir!
Let us find out his name,
And all cry, For shame!

I would not rob a bird,
Said little Mary Green;
I think I never heard
Of any thing so mean.

'T is very cruel, too,
Said little Alice Neal;
I wonder if he knew
How sad the bird would feel?

A little boy hung down his head,
And went and hid behind the bed;
For *he* stole that pretty nest
From poor little yellow-breast;
And he felt so full of shame,
He did n't like to tell his name.

MRS. CHILD

THE PRESENT.

Arrest the *present* moment; stay its flight;
Imprint the marks of wisdom on its wings:
'T is of more worth than kingdoms; far more precious
Than all the richest treasures of the earth!
O! let it not elude thy grasp; but, like
The good old pātriarch of God's holy word,
Hold the fleet āngel fast until he bless thee!

COTTON.

THE IDLE YOUNG MAN.

"THE world owes me a living." Such were the words I heard fall, the other day, from the lips of an idle young man. *The world owes you a living?* No such thing, Mr. Fold-up-your-hands! The world owes you not a single cent! You have done nothing these twenty years but consume the products earned by the sweat of other men's brows:

"You have eaten, and drunken, and slept; — what then?
Why, eaten, and drunken, and slept again."

And this is the sum total of your life! And the world, you say, "owes you a living"! For what? How came it indebted to you? What have you done for it? What family in distress have you befriended? What products have you created? What miseries have you alleviated? What errors have you removed? What arts have you perfected?

The world owes you a living, idle man? Never was there a more absurd idea! You have been a tax — a sponge upon the world ever since you came into it. It is your creditor to a vast amount. Your liabilities are immense, your assets are nothing, and yet you say the world is owing you! Go to! The amount in which you stand indebted to the world is greater than you will ever have the power to liquidate!

You owe the world the labor of your two strong arms, and all the skill in work they might have gained; you owe the world the labor of that brain of yours, the sympathies of that heart, the energies of your being; you owe the world the whole moral and intellectual capabilities of a man! Awake, then, from that dreamy, do-nothing state of slōthfulness in which you live, and let us no longer hear the assertion that the world is owing you, until you have done something to satisfy the world's just demand!

I REMEMBER, I REMEMBER.

I remember, I remember,
 The house where I was born,
The little window where the sun
 Came peeping in at morn;
He never came a wink too soon,
 Nor brought too long a day,
But now I often wish the night
 Had bōrne my breath away!

I remember, I remember,
 The roses red and white,
The violets and the lily-cups,
 Those flowers made of light!
The lilacs where the robin built,
 And where my brother set
The laburnum on his birth-day—
 The tree is living yet!

I remember, I remember,
  Where I was used to swing,
And thought the air must rush as fresh
  To swallows on the wing;
My spirit flew in feathers then,
  That is so heavy now,
And summer pools could hardly cool
  The fever on my brow!

I remember, I remember,
  The fir-trees dark and high;
I used to think their slender tops
  Were close against the sky:
It was a childish ignorance,
  But now 't is little joy
To know I 'm further off from heaven
  Than when I was a boy. HOOD.

ON THE RETURN OF BRITISH REFUGEES.

Sir, let but Liberty stretch forth her fair hand to the people of the Old World, tell them to come, and bid them welcome, and you will see them pouring in from the north and from the south, from the east and from the west; your wildernesses will be cleared and settled; your deserts will smile; your ranks will be filled; and you will soon be in a condition to defy the power of *any* adversary.

But gentlemen object to any accession from Great Britain; and particularly to the return of the British refugees. Sir, I feel no objection to the return of those deluded people. They have, to be sure, mistaken their own interests most wofully, and most wofully have they suffered the punishment due to their offenses. But the relations which we bear to them and to their native country are now changed: their king has acknowledged our independence; the quarrel is over; peace has returned, and found us a free people.

Sir, let us have the magnanimity to lay aside our antipathies and prejudices, and consider the subject in a political light. They are an enterprising, moneyed people. They will be serviceable in taking off the surplus produce of our lands, and supplying us with necessaries during the infant state of our manufactures. Even if they be inim'ical to us, in point of feeling and principle, I can see no objection, in a political view, in making them tribu'tary to our advantage. And as I have no prejudices to prevent my making use of them, so I have no fear of any mischief that they can do us. Afraid of *them!*—What! shall we, who have laid the proud British *lion* at our feet, now be afraid of his *whelps?*

P. HENRY.

THE EXCELLENT MAN.

They gave me advice and counsel in store,
Praised me and honored me, more and more;
Said that I only should "wait a while,"
Offered their patronage, too, with a smile.

But, with all their honor and approbation,
I should, long ago, have died of starvation,
Had there not come an excellent man,
Who bravely to help me along began.

Good fellow! he got me the food I ate,
His kindness and care I shall never forget;
Yet I can not embrace him, though *other* folks *can:*—
For I myself am this excellent man.

HEINE.

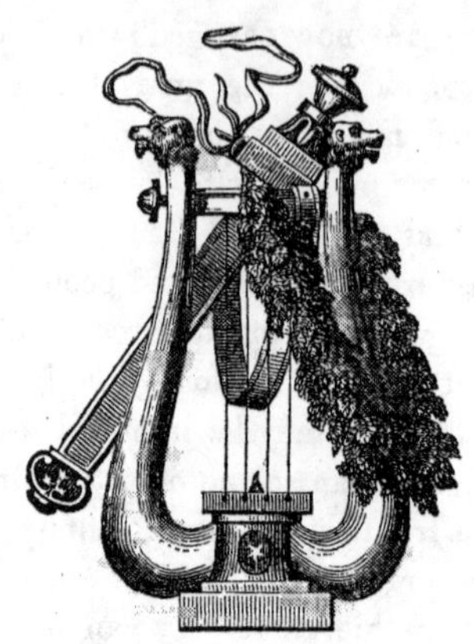

THE BATTLE OF HOHENLINDEN.

Hohenlinden is a village in Bavaria, in which a bloody battle was fought, 3d December, 1800, between the Austrians and the French.

On Linden, when the sun was low,
All bloodless lay the untrodden snow,
And dark as winter was the flow
Of Iser, rolling rapidly.

But Linden saw another sight,
When the drum beat, at dead of night,
Commanding fires of death to light
The darkness of her scenery.

By torch and trumpet fast arrayed,
Each horseman drew his battle blade,
And furious every charger neighed,
To join the dreadful revelry.

Then shook the hills with thunder riven,
Then rushed the steeds to battle driven,

And, louder than the bolts of Heaven,
    Far flashed the red artillery.

And redder yet those fires shall glow
On Linden's hills of blood-stained snow,
And darker yet shall be the flow
    Of Iser, rolling rapidly.

'T is morn, but scarce yon lurid sun
Can pierce the war-clouds, rolling dun,
Where furious Frank and fiery Hun
    Shout, in their sulphurous canopy.

The combat deepens. On, ye brave,
Who rush to glory, or the grave!
Wave, Munich, all thy banners wave!
    And charge with all thy chivalry!

Ah! few shall part where many meet!
The snow shall be their winding sheet,
And every turf, beneath their feet,
    Shall be a soldier's sepulcher.

CAMPBELL.

Iser we pronounce *E'ser; Munich, Mu'nik; chivalry, shiv'alry.*

ROLLA'S SPEECH.

My brave associates, — partners of my toil, my feelings, and my fame! — can Rolla's words add vigor to the virtuous energies which inspire your hearts? No! You have judged, as I have, the foulness of the crafty plea by which these bold invaders would delude you. Your generous spirit has compared, as mine has, the motives which, in a war like this, can animate *their* minds and *ours*. They, by a strange frenzy driven, fight for power, for plunder, and extended rule; we, for our country, our altars, and our homes. They follow an adventurer whom they fear, and obey a power which they hate; we serve a monarch whom we love — a God whom we adore.

Whene'er they move in anger, desolation tracks their progress! Whene'er they pause in amity, affliction mourns their friendship! They boast they come but to improve our state, enlarge our thoughts, and free us from the yoke of error! Yes; they will give enlightened freedom to *our* minds, who are *themselves* the slaves of passion, avarice, and pride! They offer us their protection! Yes, such protection as vultures give to lambs, covering and devouring them! They call on us to barter all of good we have inherited and proved, for the desperate chance of something better, which they promise. Be our plain answer this: The throne *we* honor is the people's choice; the laws *we* reverence are our brave fathers' legacy; the faith *we* follow teaches us to live in bonds of charity with all mankind, and die with hope of bliss beyond the grave. Tell your invaders this; and tell them, too, we seek *no* change; and, least of all, such change as *they* would bring us.

SHERIDAN.

ON THE VOWELS.

WE are little airy creatures,
All of different voice and features.
One of us in *glass* is set,
One of us you 'll find in *jet*.
T' other you may see in *tin*,
And the fourth a *box* within.
If the fifth you should pursue,
It can never fly from *you*.

SWIFT.

WHAT THE MOTHER HEARD.

As I walked over the hills, one day,
I listened, and heard a mother-sheep say:
"In all the green world there is nothing so sweet
As my little lammie with his nimble feet,
With his eyes so bright,
And his wool so white,
O, he is my darling, my heart's delight!
The robin, he
That sings in the tree,
Dearly may dote on his darlings four,
But I love my one little lambkin more."
So the mother-sheep and the little one
Side by side lay down in the sun,
And they went to sleep on the hillside warm,
While my little lammie lies here on my arm.

I went to the kitchen, and what did I see
But the old gray cat, with her kittens three:
I heard her whispering soft. Said she:
"My kittens, with tails so cunningly curled,
Are the prettiest things there can be in the world.
The bird in the tree,
And the old ewe, she
May love their babies exceedingly;
But I love my kittens from morn to night;
Which is the prettiest I can not tell, —
Which of the three, for the life of me, —
I love them all so well.
So I'll take up the kittens, the kittens I love,
And we'll lie down together, beneath the warm stove."
So the kittens lie under the stove so warm,
While my little darling lies here on my arm.

I went to the yard, and I saw the old hen
Go clucking about with her chickens ten;
And she clucked, and she scratched, and she bristled away,
And what do you think I heard the hen say?
I heard her say, "The sun never did shine
On any thing like to these chickens of mine;
You may hunt the full moon, and the stars, if you please,
But you never will find ten such chickens as these.
The cat loves her kittens, the ewe loves her lamb,
But they know not what a proud mother I am;
For lambs or for kittens I won't part with these,
Though the sheep and the cat should go down on their knees.
My dear downy darlings, my sweet little things,
Come, nestle now cosily under my wings."
So the hen said,
And the chickens sped
As fast as they could to their warm feather-bed;
And there let them lie, on their feathers so warm,
While my little chicken lies here on my arm.

I WOULD IF I COULD.

"I WOULD if I could," though much it's in use,
Is but a mistaken and sluggish excuse;
And many a person who *could* if he *would*
Is often heard saying, "I would if I could."

"Come, John," said a schoolboy, "now do not refuse,—
Come, solve me this problem,—you can if you choose."
But John at that moment was not in the mood,
And yawningly answered, "I would if I could."

At the door of a mansion, a child thinly clad,
While the cold wind blew freely, was begging for bread;

A rich man passed by her as trembling she stood, —
He answered her coldly, "I would if I could."

The scholar receiving his teacher's advice,
The swearer admonished to quit such a vice,
The child when requested to try and be good,
Oft give the same answer, — "I would if I could."

But, if we may credit what good people say,
That where a strong will is, there 's always a way,
And whatever *ought* to be *can* be and *should*,
We never need utter, "I would if I could."

OUR DUTIES TO OUR COUNTRY.

OUR proper business is improvement. Let our age be the age of improvement. In a day of peace, let us advance the arts of peace, and the works of peace. Let us develop the resources of our land, call forth its powers, build up its institutions, promote all its great interests, and see whether we also, in our day and generation, may not perform something worthy to be remembered.

Let us cultivate a true spirit of union and harmony. In pursuing the great objects which our condition points out to us, let us act under a settled conviction, and a habitual feeling, that these States are one country. Let our conceptions be enlarged to the circle of our duties. Let us extend our ideas over the whole of the vast field in which we are called to act.

Let our object be, OUR COUNTRY, OUR WHOLE COUNTRY, AND NOTHING BUT OUR COUNTRY. And, by the blessing of God, may that country itself become a vast and splendid Monument, not of oppression and terror, but of Wisdom, of Peace, and of Liberty, upon which the world may gaze, with admiration, for ever! WEBSTER.

THE EXILE OF CLOUDLAND.

When I was a dweller in Cloudland,
I dwelt in a rich and a proud land;
I was lord of the clime,
I was king of the time;
And the sun and the shower,
The leaf and the flower,
All came to my bidding in Cloudland.

I was monarch supreme in my Cloudland,
I was master of fate in that proud land;
I would not endure
That a grief without cure,
A love that could end,
Or a false-hearted friend,
Should dwell for an instant in Cloudland.

My Cloudland, my beautiful Cloudland,
I made thee a great and a proud land:
With skies ever bright,
And with hearts ever light; —
Neither sorrow nor sin
Found a harbor within,
And love was the law of my Cloudland.

But, alas for myself and my proud land!
There came revolution in Cloudland;
My people, untrue,
Broke my scepter in two,
And, false to their vow,
Took the crown from my brow,
And banished me far from my Cloudland.

My Cloudland, my beautiful Cloudland,
How happy was I in that proud land!

All the wisdom I 've won,
Since my realm was undone,
Is but poor to repay
What I lost in the day
When I turned my last looks upon Cloudland.

O, ye thoughts and ye feelings of Cloudland!
Ye died when I quitted that proud land!
I wander discrowned,
On a bare chilly ground;
An exile forlorn,
Weary, weary, and worn,
Never more to revisit my Cloudland.

BY-AND-BY.

There 's a little mischief-making
Elfin, who is ever nigh,
Thwarting every undertaking,
And his name is "By-and-By."
What we ought to do this minute
Will be better done, he 'll cry,
If to-morrow we begin it:
"Put it off," says By-and-By.

Those who heed his treacherous wooing
Will his faithless guidance rue;
What we always put off doing,
Clearly we shall never do.
We shall reach what we endeavor,
If on "Now" we more rely;
But unto the realms of "Never"
Leads the pilot By-and-By.

E. L. BLANCHARD.

THE TRUE HONOR OF A COUNTRY.

Tell me not of the honor of belonging to a free country. I ask, does our liberty bear generous fruits? Does it exalt us in manly spirit, in public virtue, above countries trodden under foot by despotism? Tell me not of the extent of our territory. I care not how large it is, if it multiply degenerate men. Speak not of our prosperity. Better be one of a poor people, plain in manners, revering God and respecting themselves, than belong to a rich country, which knows no higher good than riches.

Earnestly do I desire for this country that, instead of copying Europe with an undiscerning servility, it may have a character of its own, corresponding to the freedom and equality of our institutions. One Europe is enough. One Paris is enough. How much to be desired is it, that, separated as we are from the eastern continent by an ocean, we should be still more widely separated by simplicity of manners, by domestic purity, by inward piety, by reverence for human nature, by moral independence, by withstanding that subjection to fashion, and that debilitating sensuality, which characterize the most civilized portions of the Old World!

CHANNING.

LITTLE THINGS.

Little drops of water, little grains of sand,
Make the mighty ocean and the beauteous land:
And the little moments, humble though they be,
Make the mighty ages of eternity.
So our little errors lead the soul away
From the paths of virtue, oft in sin to stray.
Little deeds of kindness, little words of love,
Make our earth an Eden, like the heaven above.

THE WOUNDED EAGLE.

EAGLE! this is not thy sphere!
Warrior-bird, what seek'st thou here?
Wherefore by this fountain's brink
Doth thy royal pinion sink?
Wherefore on the violet's bed
Lay'st thou thus thy drooping head?
Thou that hold'st the blast in scorn,
Thou that wear'st the wings of morn!

Eagle! wilt thou not arise?
Look upon thine own bright skies!
Lift thy glance! — the fiery sun
There his pride of place hath won,
And the mountain lark is there;
And sweet sound hath filled the air.
Hast thou left that realm on high? —
O! it can be but to die!

Eagle, eagle! thou hast bowed
From thine empire o'er the cloud!
Thou that hadst ethereäl birth:
Thou hast stooped too near the earth,
And the hunter's shaft hath found thee,
And the toils of death have bound thee!
Wherefore didst thou leave thy place,
Creature of a kingly race?

Wert thou weary on thy throne?
Was the sky's dominion lone?
Chill and lone it well might be,
Yet that mighty wing was free,
Now the chain is o'er it cast,
From thy heart the blood flows fast.
Woe for gifted souls and high!
Is not such *their* destiny?

MRS. HEMANS.

The *ph* in *sphere* has the sound of *f*. *Wherefore* is pronounced *hwăr'fōr*.

THE PLEASANT HOLIDAY.

Come, my children, come away,
For the sun shines bright to-day;
Little children, come with me,
Birds, and brooks, and wild-flowers see;
Get your hats and come away,
For it is a pleasant day.

See the lambs! they sport and play
On the meadows fresh and gay;
See the kittens, full of fun,
How they frolic — how they run!
Children, too, may run and play,
For it is a pleasant day.

Bring the hoop, and bring the ball;
Come with happy faces all;
Let us make a merry ring,
Talk, and laugh, and skip, and sing!
Quickly, quickly come away,
For it is a pleasant day!

WAR INEVITABLE.

Sir, we shall not fight our battles alone. There is a just God who presides over the destinies of nations, and who will raise up friends to fight our battles for us. The battle, sir, is not to the strong alone; it is to the vigilant, the active, the brave.

Besides, sir, we have no election. If we were base enough to desire it, it is now too late to retire from the contest. There is no retreat, but in submission and slavery! Our chains are forged! Their clanking may be heard on the plains of Boston! The war is inevitable; and let it come! I repeat it, sir, let it come!

It is in vain, sir, to extenuate the matter. Gentlemen may cry, Peace, peace; but there is no peace. The war is actually begun! The next gale that sweeps from the north will bring to our ears the clash of resounding arms!

Our brethren are already in the field! Why stand we here idle? What is it that gentlemen wish? What would they have? Is life so dear, or peace so sweet, as to be purchased at the price of chains and slavery? Forbid it, Heaven! I know not what course others may take; but, as for me, give me liberty, or give me death!

PATRICK HENRY.

THE SENSES.

Say, what is it, Eyes, ye see? —
"Shade and sunshine, flower and tree;
Running waters swift and clear,
And the harvests of the year.
These we see, and for the sight
Bless the Giver infinite."

Tell me, Ears, what have ye heard? —
"Many and many a singing bird;
Winds within the tree-tops blowing;
Rapid rivers strongly flowing;
Awful thunder; ocean strong;
And the kindly human tongue.
These and more an entrance find
To the chambers of the mind."

Tell me, busy Hands, I pray,
What ye're doing through the day? —
"Ever working, never still,
We are servants to the will." —
Busy Hands, whate'er ye do,
Still keep peace and love in view.

WASHINGTON TO THE AMERICAN SOLDIERS,

BEFORE THE BATTLE OF LONG ISLAND.

Soldiers, the eyes of all our countrymen are now upon us; and we shall have their blessings and praises, if happily we are the instruments of saving them from the tyranny meditated against them. Let us, therefore, animate and encourage each other, and show the whole world that a freeman contending for liberty on his own ground is superior to any slavish mercenary on earth.

Liberty, property, life, and honor, are all at stake. Upon your courage and conduct rest the hopes of our bleeding and insulted country. Our wives, children, and parents, expect safety from us only; and they have every reason to believe that Heaven will crown with success so just a cause. The enemy will endeavor to intimidate by show and appearance; but remember they have been repulsed on various occasions by a few brave Americans. Their cause is bad; their men are conscious of it; and, if opposed with firmness and coolness on their first onset, with our advantage of works, and knowledge of the ground, the victory is most assuredly ours. Every good soldier will be silent and attentive, wait for orders, and reserve his fire until he is sure of doing execution.

THE PAPER KITE. — A Fable.

Once on a time, a paper kite
Was mounted to a wondrous height,
Where, giddy with its elevation,
It thus expressed self-admiration:
"See how yon crowds of gazing people
Admire my flight above the steeple:
How would they wonder if they knew
All that a kite like me can do!
Were I but free, I'd take a flight,
And pierce the clouds beyond their sight;
But, ah! like a poor prisoner bound,
My string confines me near the ground:
I'd brave the eagle's towering wing,
Might I but fly without my string."
It tugged and pulled, while thus it spoke,
To break the string; at last it broke:
Deprived at once of all its stay,
In vain it tried to soar away;
Unable its own weight to bear,
It fluttered downward through the air;
Unable its own course to guide,
The winds soon plunged it in the tide:
Ah, foolish kite! thou hadst no wing;
How couldst thou fly without a string?

NEWTON.

AMERICA UNCONQUERABLE.

My lords, you can not, I venture to say you can not, conquer America. Your armies in the last war effected every thing that could be effected, and what was it? My lords, you can not conquer America. What is your present situation there? We do not know the worst; but we know that in three campaigns we have done nothing, and suffered much.

As to conquest, therefore, my lords, I repeat, it is impossible. You may swell every expense and every effort still more extravagantly; pile and accumulate every assistance you can buy or borrow; traffic and barter with every little pitiful German prince, that sells and sends his subjects to the shambles of a foreign country:—your efforts are for ever im′potent and vain; doubly so from this mercenary aid on which you rely; for it irritates, to an incurable resentment, the minds of your enemies, to overrun them with the sordid sons of rapine and of plunder, — devoting them and their possessions to the rapacity of hireling cruelty.

If I were an American, as I am an Englishman, while a foreign troop was landed in my country, I never would lay down my arms, — never! never! never!

EARL OF CHATHAM.

In the Diagram at the head of this piece the figure on the left hand represents the attitude to be assumed at the passage "If I were an American," &c.; the figure on the right hand represents the attitude for the closing "never" — the arm having been brought down with energy. The first *e* in *were*, also in *therefore*, has the sound it has in *her*.

THE LOBSTERS. — A FABLE.

As a young lobster roamed about,
Itself and mother being out,
Their eyes at the same moment fell
On a boiled lobster's scarlet shell.
"Look," said the younger; "is it true
That we might wear so bright a hue?
No coral, if I trust my eye,
Can with its startling brilliance vie;
While you and I must be content
A dingy aspect to present."
"Proud, heedless fool!" the parent cried;
"Know'st thou the penalty of pride?
The tawdry finery you wish
Has ruined this unhappy fish.
The hue so much by you desired
By his destruction was acquired! —
So be contented with your lot,
Nor seek to change by going to pot."

PUNCH.

HOW TO TELL BAD NEWS.

Mr. H. HA! Steward, how are you, my old boy? How do things go on at home?

Steward. Bad enough, your honor; the magpie 's dead.

Mr. H. Poor Mag! so he 's gone. How came he to die?

Stew. Over-ate himself, sir.

Mr. H. Did he, indeed? a greedy villain! Why, what did he gĕt he liked so well?

Stew. Horse-flesh, sir; he died of eating horse-flesh?

Mr. H. How came he to get so much horse-flesh?

Stew. All your father's horses, sir.

Mr. H. What! are they dead, too?

Stew. Ay, sir; they died of over-work.

Mr. H. And why were they over-worked, pray?

Stew. To carry water, sir.

Mr. H. To carry water! and what were they carrying water for?

Stew. Sure, sir, to put out the fire.

Mr. H. Fire! what fire?

Stew. O, sir, your father's house is burned down to the ground.

Mr. H. My father's house burned down! and how came it set on fire?

Stew. I think, sir, it must have been the torches.

Mr. H. Torches! what torches?

Stew. At your mother's funeral.

Mr. H. Alas! my mother dead?

Stew. Ah, poor lady, she never looked up after it!

Mr. H. After what?

Stew. The loss of your father.

Mr. H. My father gone, too?

Stew. Yes, poor gentleman, he took to his bed as soon as he heard of it!

Mr. H. Heard of what?

Stew. The bad news, sir, and please your honor.

Mr. H. What! more miseries? more bad news? No! you can add nothing more!

Stew. Yes, sir; your bank has failed, and your credit is lost, and you are not worth a shilling in the world. I made bold, sir, to come to wait on you about it, for I thought you would like to hear the news.

I-HAVE AND O-HAD-I.

There are two little birds, quite well known in the land,—
Their names are I-Have and O-Had-I;
I-Have will come tamely and perch on your hand,
But O-Had-I will mock you most sadly.

I-Have, at first sight, is less fair to the eye,
But his worth is by far more enduring
Than a thousand O-Had-I's, that sit far and high
On roofs and on branches alluring.

Eggs of gold this I-Have by the dozen will lay,
Sweetly singing, "Content thee, content thee!"
O! merrily then will the day glide away,
And at night pleasant slumbers be sent thee.

But let an O-Had-I once ravish your eye,
And a longing to catch him once seize you,
He 'll give you no comfort nor rest till you die—
Life-long he 'll torment you and tease you.

He 'll keep you all day running up and down hill,
Now racing, now panting and creeping,
While far overland this sweet bird at his will
With his golden-tipped plumage is sweeping.

Then every wise man who attends to my song
Will count his I-Have a choice treasure,
And whene'er* an O-Had-I comes flying along,
Will just let him fly at his pleasure.

FROM THE GERMAN.

REPLY TO THE DUKE OF GRAFTON.

I AM amazed at the attack which the noble duke has made on me. Yes, my lords, I am amazed at his Grace's speech. The noble duke can not look before him, behind him, or on either side of him, without seeing some noble peer who owes his seat in this house to his successful exertions in the profession to which I belong. Does he not feel that it is as honorable to owe it to *these*, as to being the accident of an accident? To all these noble lords the language of the noble duke is as applicable and as insulting as it is to myself. But I do not fear to meet it single and alone.

No one venerates the peerage more than I do; but, my lords, I must say that the peerage solicited me, — not I the peerage. Nay, more, — I can say, and *will* say, that, as a peer of Parliament, as speaker of this right honorable house, as keeper of the great seal, as guardian of his majesty's conscience, as lord high chancellor of England, — nay, even in that character alone in which the noble duke would think it an affront to be considered, but which character none can deny me — as a man, — I am at this moment as respectable — I beg leave to add, I am as much respected — as the proudest peer I now look down upon. THURLOW.

* *E'er* and *ne'er*, contractions of *ever* and *never*, are pronounced *ăr* and *năr*, rhyming with *bare*.

"AS THY DAYS, SO SHALL THY STRENGTH BE."

PILGRIM, treading feebly on,
Smitten by the torrid sun,
Hoping for the cooling rain,
Looking for the shade in vain,
Travel-worn and faint at heart,
Weak and weary as thou art, —
Let thy spirit not repine,
Shade and shelter shall be thine;
Friendly hands to thee shall bring
Water from the cooling spring,
And the voice thou lovest best
Call the wanderer to her rest:
God hath said, to comfort thee,
"As thy day, thy strength shall be."

Christian! toiling for the prize
Kept for thee beyond the skies,

Warring with the powers of sin,
Woes without, and woes within;
Breathing now in rapture's air,
Verging then upon despair;
Trembling, hoping, filled with pain,
Then rejoicing once again, —
Shrink not from life's bitter cup,
God shall bear thy spirit up:
He shall lead thee safely on
Till the ark of rest is won —
Till thy spirit is set free:
"As thy day, thy strength shall be."

V. G. ALLYN.

THE FRACTIOUS MAN.

Mr. Cross. How now, sir? Why do you keep me knocking all day at the door?

John. I was at work, sir, in the garden. As soon as I heard your knock, I ran to open the door with such haste that I fell down.

Mr. C. No great harm was done in that. Why did n't you leave the door open?

John. Why, sir, you scolded me yesterday because I did so. When it is open, you scold; when it is shut, you scold. I should like to know what to do.

Mr. C. What to do? What to do, did you say?

John. I said it. Would you have me leave the door open?

Mr. C. No.

John. Would you have me keep it shut?

Mr. C. No.

John. But, sir, it must be either open or —

Mr. C. Don't presume to argue with me, fellow!

John. But does n't it hold to reason that a door —

Mr. C. Silence, I say!

John. And I say that a door must be either open or shut. Now, how will you have it?

Mr. C. I have told you a thousand times, you provoking fellow — I have told you that I wished it —— But what do you mean by questioning me, sir? Have you trimmed the grape-vine, as I ordered you?

John. I did that three days ago, sir.

Mr. C. Have you washed the carriage?

John. I washed it before breakfast, sir, as usual.

Mr. C. You idle, negligent fellow! — you have n't watered the horses to-day!

John. Go and see, sir, if you can make them drink any more. They have had their fill.

Mr. C. Have you given them their oats?

John. Ask William; he saw me do it.

Mr. C. But you have forgot to take the brown mare to be shod. Ah! I have you now!

John. I have the blacksmith's bill, and here it is.

Mr. C. My letters — did you take them to the post-office? Ha? You forgot that — did you?

John. Not at all, sir. The letters were in the mail ten minutes after you handed them to me.

Mr. C. How often have I told you, sir, not to scrape on that abominable violin of yours! And yet, this very morning, you —

John. This morning? You forget, sir. You broke the violin all to pieces for me last Saturday night.

Mr. C. I 'm glad of it! — Come, now; that wood which I told you to have sawed and put into the shed — why is it not done?

John. The wood is all sawed, split, and housed, sir; besides doing that, I have watered all the trees in the garden, dug over three of the beds, and was digging another when you knocked.

Mr. C. O! I must get rid of this fellow. He will plague my life out of me. Out of my sight, sir!

IMITATED FROM THE FRENCH.

RODERICK DHU AND FITZ-JAMES.

King James of Scotland, while wandering in disguise, and under the assumed name of Fitz-James, encounters Roderick Dhu, an outlaw, by the side of his watch-fire in the Highlands.

Roderick. THY name and purpose, Saxon! Stand!
Fitz-James. A stranger.
Rod. What dost thou require?
Fitz-J. Rest, and a guide, and food, and fire.
My life 's beset, my path is lost,
The gale has chilled my limbs with frost.
Rod. Art thou a friend to Roderick?
Fitz-J. No.
Rod. Thou darest not call thyself a foe?
Fitz-J. I dare! to him and all the band
He brings to aid his murderous hand.
Rod. Bold words! But, if I mark aright,
Thou bear'st the belt and spur of knight.
Fitz-J. Then by these tokens may'st thou know
Each proud oppressor's mortal foe!
Rod. Enough, enough! Sit down and share
A soldier's couch, a soldier's fare.

SIR WALTER SCOTT.

ALEXANDER THE GREAT AND THE ROBBER.

Alexander. WHAT! Art thou the Thracian robber, of whose ex-ploits' I have heard so much?

Robber. I am a Thracian, and a soldier.

Alex. A soldier? A thief, a plunderer, an assassin! the pest of the country! I could honor thy courage, but I must detest and punish thy crimes.

Rob. What have I done, of which you can complain?

Alex. Hast thou not set at defiance my authority, violated the public peace, and passed thy life in injuring the persons and properties of thy fellow-subjects?

Rob. Alexander! I am your captive; I must hear what you please to say, and endure what you please to inflict. But my soul is unconquered; and if I reply at all to your reproaches, I will reply like a free man.

Alex. Speak freely. Far be it from me to take the advantage of my power to silence those with whom I deign to converse.

Rob. I must then answer your question by another. How have you passed your life?

Alex. Like a hero. Ask Fame, and she will tell you. Among the brave, I have been the bravest; among sovereigns, the noblest; among conquerors, the mightiest.

Rob. And does not Fame speak of me, too? Was there ever a bolder captain of a more valiant band? Was there ever —— But I scorn to boast. You yourself know that I have not been easily subdued.

Alex. Still, what are you but a robber — a base, dishonest robber?

Rob. And what is a conqueror? Have not you, too, gone about the earth like an evil genius, blasting the fair fruits of peace and industry, plundering, ravaging, killing, without law, without justice, merely to gratify an insatiable lust for dominion? All that I have done to a single district with a hundred followers, you have done to whole nations with a hundred thousand. If I have stripped individuals, you have ruined kings and princes. If I have burnt a few hamlets, you have desolated the most flourishing kingdoms and cities of the earth. What is, then, the difference, but that, as you were born a king, and I a private man, you have been able to become a mightier robber than I?

Alex. But, if I have taken like a king, I have given like a king. If I have subverted empires, I have founded greater. I have cherished arts, commerce, and philosophy.

Rob. I, too, have freely given to the poor what I took from the rich. I have established order and discipline among the most ferocious of mankind, and have stretched out my protecting arm over the oppressed. I know, indeed, little of the philosophy you talk of, but I believe neither you nor I shall ever atone to the world for half the mischief we have done it.

Alex. Leave me. (*He speaks as if to persons off the stage.*) Take off his chains, and use him well. — Are we, then, so much alike? Alexander like a robber! Let me reflect.

DR. AIKIN.

CONTENTED JOHN.

ONE honest John Tomkins, a hedger and ditcher,
Although he was poor, did not want to be richer;
For all such vain wishes in him were prevented,
By a fortunate habit of being contented.

Though cold was the weather, or dear was the food,
John never was found in a murmuring mood;
For this he was constantly heard to declare —
What he could not prevent, he would cheerfully bear.

"For why should I grumble and murmur?" he said;
"If I can not get meat, I can surely get bread;
And though fretting may make my calamities deeper,
It never can cause bread and cheese to be cheaper."

If John was afflicted with sickness and pain,
He wished himself better, but did not complain,
Nor lie down to fret in despondence and sorrow,
But said — that he hoped to be better to-morrow.

If any one wronged him, or treated him ill,
Why, John was good-natured and sociable still;
For he said — that revenging the injury done,
Would be making two rogues, when there need be but one.

And thus honest John, though his station was humble,
Passed through this sad world without even a grumble;
And I wish that some folks, who are greater and richer,
Would copy John Tomkins, the hedger and ditcher.

THE MIMIC.

A MIMIC I knew, who, to give him his due,
Was exceeded by none and was equaled by few.

He could bark like a dog; he could grunt like a hog;
Nay, I really believe he could croak like a frog.

Then, as for a bird, — you may trust to my word,
'T was the best imitation that ever you heard.

It must be confessed that he copied birds best;
You 'd have thought he had lived all his life in a nest.

It happened, one day, that he came in the way
Of a sportsman — an excellent marksman, they say.

And near a stone wall, with his little bird-call,
The mimic attempted to imitate all.

So well did he do it, the birds all flew to it;
But, ah! he had certainly reason to rue it.

It turned out no fun, — for, the man with the gun,
Who was seeking for partridges, took him for one.

He was shot in the side; and he feelingly cried,
A moment or so ere he fainted and died:

"Who for others prepare a trap, should beware
They do not themselves fall into the snare."

THE LESSON OF LOVE.

Be not harsh and unforgiving;
Live in love, — 't is pleasant living!
If an angry man should meet thee,
And assail thee indiscreetly,
Turn not thou again and rend him,
Lest thou needlessly offend him:
Show him love hath been thy teacher —
Kindness is a potent preacher;
Gentleness is e'er forgiving;
Live in love, — 't is pleasant living!

Why be angry with each other?
Man was made to love his brother;
Kindness is a human duty, —
Meekness a celestial beauty.
Words of kindness, if in season,
Have a weight with men of reason.
Don't be others' follies blaming,
And their little vices naming;
Charity 's a cure for railing,
Suffers much, — is all-prevailing.
Courage, then! and be forgiving;
Live in love, — 't is pleasant living!

Hast thou known that bitter feeling
Gendered by our hate's concealing?
Better love, though e'er so blindly, —
Better banish thoughts unkindly.
Words are wind: O! let them never
Friendship's golden love-cord sever!
Nor be angry, though another
Fail to treat thee like a brother: —
"Brother," say, "let 's be forgiving!
Live in love, — 't is pleasant living!"

THE QUARREL OF THE AUTHORS.

1st. Sir, I 'm proud to have met you; long have I known
Your productions, and wished them (how often!) my own.
Your verses have beauties in none other found.

2d. In *yours*, sir, the Loves and the Graces abound.

1st. Your phrases are neat, your style charmingly light.

2d. We find the pathetic in all that you write.

1st. How sweet your Bu-col'ics! how tender and true!
The-oc'ri-tus, surely, was nothing to you.

2d. Your odes have a noble and elegant vein,
That even old Horace could never attain.
1st. Can any thing equal your love-ditties rare?
2d. Can aught with your wonderful sonnets compare?
1st. If the public could estimate half of your worth, —
2d. If merit now met its due honors on earth, —
1st. You would roll through the streets in a carriage of gold.
2d. Every square in the city your statue would hold.
Hem! this ballad of mine (*unrolling a manuscript*) — your opinion upon it.
I should like to —
1st. Pray, sir, have you met with a sonnet
On the meeting of Congress —
2d. A sonnet? Just so;
'T was read at a party a few nights ago.
1st. Do you know who 's the author?
2d. I know not — nor care;
For 't is an exceedingly trifling affair.
1st. Yet many admire it — or so they tell *me*.
2d. No matter for that, it 's as bad as can be;
And if you had but seen it, sir, you 'd think so too.
1st. Dear sir, I am sorry to differ from you;
But I hold that its merit must every one strike.
2d. May the Muses preserve me from making the like!
1st. (*Angrily.*) I maintain that a better the world cannot show:
For *I* am the author — yes, *I*, you must know.
2d. You?
1st. I.
2d. Well, I wonder how that came to pass.
1st. I had the bad luck not to please you, alas!
2d. Perhaps there was something distracted my head;
Or else the man spoiled it, so badly he read.
But here is my ballad, concerning which, I —
1st. The days of the ballad, methinks, are gone by;
'T is very old-fashioned, and out of date quite.
2d. Yet, even now, many in ballads delight.
1st. No matter; I think them decidedly flat.

2d. *You* think them! Perhaps they 're no worse, sir, for that.
1st. For pedants, indeed, they have charms beyond measure.
2d. And yet we perceive that they give *you* no pleasure.
1st. You give others qualities found but in *you*.
2d. You call others names that are justly *your* due.
Go, blotter of foolscap! contemptible creature!
1st. Go, scribbler of sonnets, and butcher of meter!
2d. Go, impudent pla'giarist! — pedant, gĕt out!
1st. Go, rascal — be careful! mind what you 're about.
2d. Go, go! strip your writings of each borrowed plume;
Let the Greeks and the Latins their beauties resume.
1st. Go, you, and ask pardon of Venus and Bacchus,
For your lame imitations of jolly old Flaccus.
2d. Remember your book's insignificant sale.
1st. Remember your bookseller driven to jail.
2d. My pen shall avenge me, — to your great disaster.
1st. And mine shall let *you* know, sir, who is your master.
2d. I defy you in verse, prose, Latin, and Greek!
1st. You shall hear from me, sir, in the course of the week.

IMITATED FROM MOLIÈRE.

KINDNESS.

A LITTLE spring had lost its way
Amid the grass and fern;
A passing stranger scooped a well,
Where weary men might turn;
He walled it in, and hung, with care,
A ladle at the brink;
He thought not of the deed he did,
But judged that Toil might drink.
He passed again — and, lo! the well,
By summers never dried,
Had cooled ten thousand parchĕd tongues,
And saved a life beside.

"If they fall, we fall with them."

OUR DUTIES AS AMERICANS.

It can not be denied, but by those who would dispute against the sun, that *with* America, and *in* America, a new era commences in human affairs. This era is distinguished by free representative governments, by entire religious liberty, by improved systems of national intercourse, by a newly awakened and an unconquerable spirit of free inquiry, and by a diffusion of knowledge through the community, such as has been before altogether unknown and unheard of. America, America, our country, fellow-citizens, our own dear and native land, is inseparably connected, fast bound up, in fortune and by fate, with these great interests. *If they fall, we fall with them;* if they stand, it will be because we have maintained them.

Let us con-tem'plate, then, this connection, which binds the prosperity of others to our own; and let us manfully discharge all the duties which it imposes. If we cherish the virtues and the principles of our fathers, Heaven will assist us to carry on the work of human liberty and human happiness. Auspicious omens cheer us. Great examples are before us. Our own firmament now shines brightly upon our path. WASHINGTON is in the clear upper sky. These other stars have now joined the American constellation; they circle round their center, and the heavens beam with new light. Beneath this illumination let us walk the course of life, and at its close devoutly commend our beloved country, the common parent of us all, to the Divine Benignity.

WEBSTER.

HARRY'S TERRIBLE ADVENTURE.

THE night was dark, the sun was hid
Beneath the mountain gray;
And not a single star appeared,
To shoot a friendly ray.

Across the heath the owlet flew,
And screamed along the blast,
As onward, with a quickened step,
Benighted Harry passed.

At intervals, amid the gloom
A flash of lightning played,
And showed the ruts with water filled,
Beside the hedge's shade.

Again in thickest darkness plunged,
He groped his way to find;

And now he thought he spied beyond
  A form of dreadful kind.

In shadowy white it upward rose,
  Of dress or mantle bare,
And stretched its naked arms as if
  To catch him by the hair.

Poor Harry felt his blood run cold,
  At what before him stood:
Yet like a man he then resolved
  To do the best he could.

So, calling all his courage up,
  He to the figure went;
And through the găthering gloom of night
  His piercing eyes he bent.

But when he came quite near the ghost
  That gave him such a fright,
He clapped together both his hands,
  And loudly laughed outright.

For there a guide-post good he found,
  The stranger's road to mark;
A pleasant sprite was this to see,
  For Harry in the dark!

"Well done!" said he; "one thing, at least,
  I've learned, beyond a doubt, —
Whatever frightens me again,
  I'll try to find it out.

"And when I hear an idle tale
  Of any shocking ghost,
I'll tell of this, my lonely walk,
  And of the tall white guide-post."

AN APPEAL TO ARMS.

I HAVE but one lamp by which my feet are guided, and that is the lamp of experience. I know of no way of judging of the future but by the past. And, judging by the past, I wish to know what there has been in the conduct of the British ministry, for the last ten years, to justify those hopes with which gentlemen have been pleased to solace themselves and the house. Is it that insidious smile with which our petition has been lately received? Trust it not, sir! It will prove a *snare* to your feet. Suffer not yourselves to be betrayed with a kiss!

Let us not, I beseech you, deceive ourselves longer. We have done every thing that could be done to avert the storm which is now coming on. We have petitioned — we have remonstrated — we have supplicated — we have prostrated ourselves before the throne, and have implored its interposition to arrest the tyrannical hands of the ministry and Parliament. Our petitions have been slighted; our remonstrances have produced additional violence and insult; our supplications have been disregarded; and we have been spurned, with contempt, from the foot of the throne.

In vain, after these things, may we indulge the fond hope of peace and reconciliation. There is no longer any room for hope. If we wish to be free, — if we mean to preserve inviolate those inestimable privileges for which we have been so long contending, — if we mean not basely to abandon the noble struggle in which we have been so long engaged, and which we have pledged ourselves never to abandon, until the glorious object of our contest shall be obtained, — we must fight! — I repeat it, sir, we must fight! An appeal to arms, and to the God of Hosts, is all that is left us!

PATRICK HENRY.

NERO.

A NOBLE dog our Nero was;
He came from Newfoundland;
The children all could play with him,
And pat him with the hand.

A thick and shaggy wool he had,
That guarded him from cold;
His feet were broad and stout, and he
Was kind as he was bold.

If any quarrel-seeking cur
Rushed at him for a fight,
And Nero did but look at him,
The cur would run, in fright.

One day our little sister Ruth
Fell over from a boat;
But Nero was on board, and he
Was speedily afloat.

He swam to where her sinking form,
  Swept by a wave, was seen;
He seized the collar of her dress
  His good strong teeth between.

He bore her up — he brought her through
  The salt waves to our side;
We took her in — "The darling 's safe!
  Brave dog!" my father cried.

No wonder that we love to play
  With such a dog as Nero;
Better a medal he deserves,
  Than many a fighting hero. OSBORNE.

In the word *Newfoundland* put the accent on the last syllable. Give the *oa* in *boat* and *coat* the full sound of long *o*, as in *go*. Do not pronounce *medal* as if it were *meddle:* the *a* has a slightly obscured sound of short *a*. Sound the *h* in *humble*, *exhibit*, &c. Sound the *ir* in *first* and the *ur* in *burst* like *er* in *her*.

UNRIGHTEOUS MEASURES AGAINST AMERICA.

My lords, who is the man that, in addition to the disgraces and mischiefs of our armies, has dared to associate with our arms the tomahawk and scalping-knife of the savage? — to call into civilized alliance the wild and inhuman savage of the woods; to delegate to the merciless Indian the defense of disputed rights; and to wage the horrors of his barbarous war against our brĕthren? These enormities cry aloud for redress and punishment; and, unless thoroughly done away, they will be an indelible stain on the national character.

It is not the least of our misfortunes that the strength and character of our army are thus impaired. Familiarized to horrid scenes of savage cruelty, it can no longer boast the generous principles which dignify a soldier; no longer feel "the pride, pomp, circumstance of glorious war, that make ambition virtue." What makes ambition virtue? The sense of honor! But is the sense of honor consistent with a spirit of plunder, or the practice of murder?

My lords, you can not conciliate America by your present measures; you can not *subdue* her by your *present*, or by *any* measures. In a just and necessary war, to maintain the rights or honor of my country, I would strip the shirt from my back to support it. But in such a war as this, unjust in its principle, impracticable in its means, and ruinous in its consequences, I would not contribute a single effort, nor a single shilling.

EARL OF CHATHAM.

BRUCE TO HIS TROOPS.

Scots! who have with Wallace bled,
Scots! whom Bruce has often led,
Welcome to your gory bed,
Or to victory.

Now's the day, and now's the hour,
See the front of battle lower!
See approach proud Edward's power —
Chains and slavery!

Who will be a traitor knave?
Who can fill a coward's grave?
Who so base as be a slave?
Let him turn and flee!

Who for Scotland's king and law
Freedom's sword will strongly draw,
Freeman stand, or freeman fall,
Let him follow me!

By oppression's woes and pains,
By your sons in servile chains,
We will drain our dearest veins,
But they shall be free!

Lay the proud usurpers low!
Tyrants fall in every foe!
Liberty 's in every blow!—
Let us do or die! BURNS.

WATER, BRIGHT WATER FOR ME!

O! WATER for me! bright water for me,
And wine for the tremulous debauchee!
It cooleth the brow, it cooleth the brain,
It maketh the faint one strong again;
It comes o'er the sense like a breeze from the sea,
All freshness, like infant purity;
O! water, bright water, for me, for me!
Give wine, give wine to the debauchee!

Fill to the brim! Fill, fill to the brim!
For water strengtheneth life and limb;
To the days of the agëd it addeth length;
To the might of the strong it addeth strength;
It freshens the heart, it brightens the sight,
'T is quaffing a goblet of morning light.
So, water, I will drink naught but thee,
Thou parent of health and energy! E. JOHNSON.

OLD GRIMES.

Old Grimes is dead! that good old man
  We never shall see more;
He used to wear a long black coat,
  All buttoned down before.

His heart was open as the day,
  His feelings all were true;
His hair was some inclined to gray —
  He wore it in a queue.

Whene'er he heard the voice of pain,
  His breast with pity burned;
The large round head upon his cane
  From ivory was turned.

Kind words he ever had for all;
  He knew no base design;
His eyes were dark and rather small,
  His nose was aquiline.

He lived at peace with all mankind;
  In friendship he was true;
His coat had pocket-holes behind;
  His pantaloons were blue.

Unharmed, the sin which earth pollutes
  He passed securely o'er;
And never wore a pair of boots
  For thirty years or more.

But good old Grimes is now at rest,
  Nor fears Misfortune's frown;
He wore a double-breasted vest —
  The stripes ran up and down.

He modest merit sought to find,
And pay it its desert;
He had no malice in his mind,
No ruffles on his shirt.

His neighbors he did not abuse —
Was sociable and gay;
He wore large buckles on his shoes,
And changed them every day.

His knowledge, hid from public gaze,
He did not bring to view;
Nor make a noise, town-meeting days,
As many people do.

His worldly goods he never threw
In trust to fortune's chances;
But lived (as all his brothers do)
In easy circumstances.

Thus undisturbed by anxious cares
His peaceful moments ran;
And everybody said he was
A fine old gentleman.

ALBERT G. GREENE.

SPEECH OF MIN-NE-VAH, AN INDIAN CHIEF.

White men, we give way before you, like the driving mist before the gale. The next new moon shall not find one of our tribe on these forsaken hunting-grounds. You have conquered. We confess that we are the weaker party. We can not stay here, if we would.

But do not think, my white brethren, that it is your courage which has brought us low. Your swords are sharp, and your rifles are true; but they did not do the work of our degradation and subjection. You brought a surer, a deadlier weapon for our destruction. You brought the whiskey-bottle, my white brethren. That has done for us what steel and powder could not do. It has wasted us as April suns waste the snow on the hill-tops. It has taken the wisdom out of the brains of our old men, and the manhood out of the limbs of our young warriors. It has made us bad hunters, bad husbands, bad fathers, bad Indians, bad men. When we are settled in our distant hunting-grounds, grant us one favor, at least — keep your accursed fire-water from our lips. We may yet be men and warriors, without that. But, with it, — war, famine, and disease, shall soon finish the work of extermination which ye have begun.

WARREN TO HIS MEN AT BUNKER HILL.

STAND! the ground 's your own, my braves!
Will ye give it up to slaves?
Will ye look for greener graves?
Hope ye mercy still?
What 's the mercy despots feel? —
Hear it in that battle-peal!
Read it on yon bristling steel!
Ask it — ye who will.

Fear ye foes who kill for hire?
Will ye to your *homes* retire?
Look behind you! they 're on fire! *
And, before you, see
Who have done it! — From the vale
On they come! — and will ye quail? —

* The British set fire to Charlestown, which is within sight of Bunker Hill, just before the battle.

Leaden rain and iron hail
    Let their welcome be!

In the God of battles trust!
Die we may — and die we must: —
But, O! where can dust to dust
    Be consigned so well,
As where heaven its dews shall shed
On the martyred pātriot's bed,
And the rocks shall rear their head,
    Of his deeds to tell! PIERPONT.

LIFE WITHOUT FREEDOM.

From life without freedom, say, who would not fly?
For one day of freedom, O! who would not die?
Hark! — hark! 't is the trumpet! the call of the brave,
The death-song of tyrants, the dirge of the slave.
Our country lies bleeding — haste, haste to her aid;
One arm that defends is worth hosts that invade.

In death's kindly bosom our last hope remains —
The dead fear no tyrants, the grave has no chains.
On, on to the combat! the heroes that bleed
For virtue and country are heroes indeed.
And, O! even if Freedom from *this* world be driven,
Despair not — at least we shall find her in heaven!

MOORE.

AGAINST CIVIL DISCORD.

I have been charged with ambition. Yes, I *have* ambition; but it is the ambition of being the humble instrument in the hands of Providence to reconcile a distracted people; once more to revive concord and harmony in a distracted land, — the pleasing ambition of contem'plating the glorious spectacle of a free, united, prosperous, and fraternal people!

If there be any who want civil war, — who want to see the blood of any portion of our countrymen spilt, — I am not one of them. I wish to see war of no kind; but, above all, do I not desire to see a *civil* war.

When war begins, whether civil or foreign, no human foresight is competent to foresee when, or how, or where, it is to terminate. But when a civil war shall be lighted up in the bosom of our own happy land, and armies are marching, and commanders are winning their victories, and fleets are in motion on our coast, — tell me, if you can — tell me, if any human being can tell, its duration! CLAY.

THE JUVENILE ORATOR.

You 'd scarce expect one of my age
To speak in public, on the stage;
And if I chance to fall below
De-mos'the-nēs or Cicero,
Don't view me with a critic's eye,
But pass my imperfections by.
Large streams from little fountains flow;
Tall oaks from little acorns grow:
And though I now am small and young,
Of judgment weak, and feeble tongue,
Yet all great learnëd men, — like me
Once learned to read their A, B, C.
And why may not Columbia's soil
Rear men as great as Britain's isle;
Exceed what Greece and Rome have done,
Or any land beneath the sun?
May n't Massachusetts prove as great
As any other sister state?

Or, where 's the town, go far and near,
That does not find a rival here?
Or, where 's the boy but three feet high
Who 's made improvements more than I?
These thoughts inspire my youthful mind
To be the greatest of mankind;
Great, not like Cæsar, stained with blood;
But only great, as I am good.

DAVID EVERETT.

Do not pronounce *soil* to rhyme with *isle*; but give the *oi* its true sound, as in *coin*.

LIBERTY AND UNION.

When my eyes shall be turned to behold for the last time the sun in heaven, may I not see him shining on the broken and dishonored fragments of a once glorious Union; on states dissevered, discordant, belligerent; on a land rent with civil feuds, or drenched, it may be, in fraternal blood! Let their last feeble and lingering glance rather behold the gorgeous ensign of the republic, now known and honored throughout the earth, still full high advanced, its arms and trophies streaming in their original luster, not a stripe erased or polluted, not a single star obscured, bearing for its motto no such miserable interrog'atory as, "What is all this worth?" nor those other words of delusion and folly, "Liberty first, and union afterward;" but everywhere spread all over in characters of light, blazing on all its ample folds, as they float over the sea and over the land, and in every wind under the whole heavens, that other sentiment, dear to every true American heart, — Liberty *and* union, now and for ever, one and inseparable!

WEBSTER.

PARAPHRASE OF THE NINETEENTH PSALM.

The spacious firmament on high,
With all the blue ethereäl sky,
And spangled heavens, a shining frame,
Their great Original proclaim:
The unwearied sun, from day to day,
Does his Creator's power display,
And publishes to every land
The work of an Almighty Hand.

Soon as the evening shades prevail,
The moon takes up the wondrous tale,
And nightly, to the listening earth,
Repeats the story of her birth;

Whilst all the stars that round her burn,
And all the planets, in their turn,
Confirm the tidings as they roll,
And spread the truth from pole to pole.

What though, in solemn silence, all
Move round this dark terrestrial ball!
What though no real voice, nor sound,
Amid their radiant orbs be found!
In Reason's car they all rejoice,
And utter forth a glorious voice,
For ever singing, as they shine,
"The Hand that made us is Divine."

ADDISON.

THE FARMER AND THE LANDLORD.

A farmer, of an honest fame,
One morning to his landlord came:
"Alas, my lord," he weeping said,
"Gored by my bull, your ox is dead.
What must be done?"—"The case is plain,"
Replies the lord; "the creature slain,
The owner of the bull must pay;
Let it be done without delay."—
"Heaven give your worship long to live!
I hope you will a good ox give,
For mine was good!"—"How! *yours*, my friend?
Let me your story comprehend:
Your bull, you say, my ox has gored?"—
"Forgive me the mistake, my lord,
In my confusion I have made;
Mine was the ox, I should have said;

But 't is all one; what 's just for me,
Must justice for your worship be:
I 'll tell the steward what you say." —
"Not yet! We 'll think of 't; go your way;
Further inquiry must be had;
Perhaps your fences were but bad;
Perhaps — But come again to-morrow."
The honest laborer saw, with sorrow,
That justice wears a different face,
When for themselves men put the case.

BOOTHBY.

LOGAN, AN INDIAN CHIEF, TO LORD DUNMORE.

I APPEAL to any white man to say, if ever he entered Logan's cabin hungry, and he gave him not meat; if ever he came cold and naked, and he clothed him not. During the course of the last long and bloody war, Logan remained idle in his cabin, an advocate for peace. Such was my love for the whites, that my countrymen pointed at me as they passed, and said, "Logan is the friend of white men." I had even thought to have lived with you, but for the injuries of one man. Colonel Cresap, the last spring, in cold blood, and unprovoked, murdered all the relations of Logan, not sparing even my women and children. There runs not a drop of my blood in the veins of any living creature. This called on me for revenge. I have sought it. I have killed many. I have glutted my vengeance. For my country, I rejoice at the beams of peace. But do not think that mine is the joy of fear. Logan never felt fear. Logan will not turn on his heel to save his life. Who is there to mourn for Logan? Not one!

THE SNOW-HUT.

THE welcome snow! the feathery snow!
How fast to the ground the little flakes go!
They have covered the top of the hill with white,
They have hidden the garden-hedge from sight,
They have powdered the trees, and woven a woof
Of ermine for every shed and roof;
They have spread a sheet in the valley's lap,
And put on the post at the gate a cap.

In his kennel yonder old Nero lay
While the drifts swept over and far away;
And when he woke up he found it was dark.
Odd enough! thought he, beginning to bark;
Then we, with our shovels of every shape,
Helped the old fellow out of his scrape.

Well powdered, he scrambled out, at length,
And shook his old jacket with all his strength.

Take your spade, brother, and I will show
How the Esquimaux live in their hovels of snow;
We 'll dig us a hole where we bōth can creep,
And sheltered from cold lie down to sleep.
We 'll have us a window made of ice,
And make our floor all level and nice:
And I will show you how Kane and his men
Lay snug on the snow in their Arctic den.

Pronounce *Esquimaux* as if it were *Es'ke-mo*. The *o* in *hovel* has its short sound, as in *nŏvel;* but in *shovel, o* has the sound of short *u*, as in *but*.

YOUTHFUL PIETY.

By cool Si-lo'am's shady rill,
 How sweet the lily grows!
How sweet the breath beneath the hill
 Of Sharon's dewy rose!

Lo! such the child whose early feet
 The paths of peace have trod;
Whose secret heart with influence sweet
 Is upward drawn to God.

By cool Si-lo'am's shady rill,
 The lily must decay;
The rose that blooms beneath the hill
 Must shortly fade away:

And soon, too soon, the wintry hour
 Of man's maturer age
Will shake the soul with Sorrow's power,
 And stormy Passion's rage.

O! Thou, whose infant feet were found
Within thy Father's shrine,
Whose years, with changeless virtue crowned,
Were all alike divine,—

Dependent on thy bounteous breath,
We seek thy grace alone,
In childhood, manhood, age, and death,
To keep us still thine own. HEBER.

THE DEPARTING SWALLOWS.

Ye gentle birds, that perch aloof,
And smooth your pinions on my roof,
Preparing for departure hence,
Now Winter's angry threats commence,—
Like you, my soul would smooth her plume
For longer flights beyond the tomb.

May God, by whom is seen and heard
Departing man and wandering bird,
In mercy mark us for his own,
And guide us to the land unknown!

WILLIAM HAYLEY.

TRUE COMELINESS.

What is the blooming tincture of the skin,
To peace of mind and harmony within?
What the bright sparkling of the finest eye
To the soft soothing of a calm reply?
Can comeliness of form, or shape, or air,
With comeliness of words or deeds compare?
No! those at first the unwary heart may gain,
But these, these only, can the heart retain. GAY.

THE DYING CHIEF.

The stars looked down on the battle-plain,
  Where night-winds were deeply sighing,
And with shattered blade, near his war-steed slain,
  Lay a youthful chieftain dying.

Proudly he lay on his broken shield,
  By the rushing Guadalquivir,
While, dark with the blood of his last red field,
  Swept on the majestic river.

There were hands which came to bind his wound,
  There were eyes o'er the warrior weeping;
But he raised his head from the dewy ground,
  Where the land's high hearts were sleeping!

And "Away!" he cried, "your aid is vain,
  My soul may not brook recalling;
I have seen the stately flower of Spain
  As the autumn vine-leaves falling!

"I have seen the Moorish banners wave
O'er the halls where my youth was cherished;
I have drawn a sword that could not save,
I have stood where my king hath perished!

"Leave me to die with the free and brave,
On the banks of my own bright river!
Ye can give me naught but a warrior's grave
By the chainless Guadalquivir!"

THE PILOT.

"O, PILOT! 't is a fearful night,
There 's danger on the deep;
I 'll come and pace the deck with thee,—
I do not care to sleep."
"Go down," the sailor cried, "go down;
This is no place for thee;
Fear not! but trust in Providence,
Wherever thou mayest be."

"Ah, Pilot, dangers often met
We all are apt to slight,
And thou hast known these raging waves
But to subdue their might."
"It is not apathy," he cried,
"That gives this strength to me;
Fear not! but trust in Providence,
Wherever thou mayest be.

"On such a night the sea engulfed
My father's lifeless form;
My only brother's boat went down,
In just so wild a storm;

And such, perhaps, may be my fate —
  But still I say to thee,
Fear not! but trust in Providence,
  Wherever thou mayest be."

T. H. BAYLY.

THE AMERICAN UNION.

Thou, too, sail on, O Ship of State!
Sail on, O Union, strong and great!
Humanity, with all its fears,
With all its hopes of future years,
Is hanging breathless on thy fate!
We know what master laid thy keel,
What workmen wrought thy ribs of steel,
Who made each mast, and sail, and rope,
What anvils rang, what hammers beat,
In what a forge and what a heat
Were shaped the anchors of thy hope!

Fear not each sudden sound and shock, —
'T is of the wave, and not the rock;
'T is but the flapping of the sail,
And not a rent made by the gale!

In spite of rock and tempest's roar,
In spite of false lights on the shore,
Sail on, nor fear to breast the sea!
Our hearts, our hopes, are all with thee:
Our hearts, our hopes, our prayers, our tears,
Our faith triumphant o'er our fears,
Are all with thee — are all with thee!

LONGFELLOW.

THE BIRD TO THE SPORTSMAN.

Wouldst thou have me fall, or fly?
Hear me sing, or see me die?
If thy heart is cold and dull,
Knowing nothing beautiful, —
If thy proud eye never glows
With the light love only knows, —
If the loss of friends or home
Ne'er hath made life wearisome, —
If thy cheek has never known
Tears that fall with sorrow's moan, —
If a hopeless mother's sigh
Brings no tear-drop from thine eye,
Thou may'st smile to see me die.

But, if thou canst love the lay
Welcoming the birth of May, —
Or summer's song, or autumn's dirge,
Cheering winter's dreary verge, —
If thou lovest Beauty's hues,
Decked with light or gemmed with dews, —
If, all meaner thoughts above,
Thou canst hope, and trust, and love, —
If, from all dishonor free,
Thou canst Nature's lover be, —
Spare her minstrels — pity me!

PLEASURES THAT DO NOT FAIL.

There are pleasures that time will not take away. While animal spirits fail, and joys which depend upon the liveliness of the passions decline with years, the solid comforts of a holy life, the delights of virtue and a good conscience, will be a new source of happiness in old age, and have a charm for the end of life.

As the stream flows pleasantest when it approaches the ocean; as the flowers send up their sweetest odors at the close of day; as the sun appears with greatest beauty in his going down; so, at the end of his career, the virtues and graces of a good man's life come before him with the most delightful remembrance, and impart a joy which he never felt before. Over all the moments of life religion scatters her favors, but reserves her best, her choicest, her divinest blessings, for the last hour.

LOGAN.

NOT TO MYSELF ALONE.

"Not to myself alone,"
The little opening flower, transported, cries, —
"Not to myself alone I bud and bloom;
With fragrant breath the breezes I perfume,
And gladden all things with my rainbow dyes;
The bee comes sipping, every eventide,
His dainty fill;
The butterfly within my cup doth hide
From threatening ill."

"Not to myself alone,"
The circling star with honest pride doth boast, —
"Not to myself alone I rise and set;
I write upon night's coronal of jet
His power and skill who formed our myriad host;
A friendly bēacon at Heaven's open gate,
I gem the sky,
That man may ne'er forget, in every fate,
His home on high."

"Not to myself alone,"
The heavy-laden bee doth murmuring hum, —
"Not to myself alone from flower to flower
I rove the wood, the garden, and the bower,
And to the hive at evening weary come;
For man, for man the luscious food I pile
With busy care,
Content if he repay my ceaseless toil
With scanty share."

"Not to myself alone,"
The soaring bird with lusty pinion sings, —
"Not to myself alone I raise my song;
I cheer the drooping with my warbling tongue,
And bear the mourner on my viewless wings;
I bid the hymnless churl my anthem learn,
And God adore;
I call the worldling from his drŏss to turn,
And sing and soar."

"Not to myself alone,"
The streamlet whispers on its pebbly way, —
"Not to myself alone I sparkling glide;
I scatter health and life on every side,
And strew the fields with herb and flow'ret gay;
I sing unto the common, bleak and bare,
My gladsome tune;
I sweeten and refresh the languid air
In droughty June."

"Not to thyself alone!" —
O! man, forget not thou, — earth's honored priest,
Its tongue, its soul, its life, its pulse, its heart —
In earth's great chorus to sustain *thy* part.

Chiefest of guests at Love's ungrudging feast,
Play not the niggard; spurn thy native clod,
And *self* disown;
Live to thy neighbor, — live unto thy God, —
Not to thyself alone!

BRUTUS ON THE DEATH OF CÆSAR.

Romans, countrymen, and lovers! Hear me for my cause; and be silent that you may hear. Believe me for mine honor; and have respect to mine honor, that you may believe. Censure me in your wisdom, and awake your senses that you may the better judge. If there be any in this assembly, — any dear friend of Cæsar's, — to him I say, that Brutus' love to Cæsar was not less than his. If, then, that friend demand why Brutus rose against Cæsar, this is my answer: Not that I loved Cæsar less, but that I loved Rome more. Had you rather Cæsar were living, and die all slaves, than that Cæsar were dead, to live all freemen? As Cæsar loved me, I weep for him; as he was fortunate, I rejoice at it; as he was valiant, I honor him; but as he was ambitious, I slew him! There are tears for his love; joy for his fortune; honor for his valor; and death for his ambition! SHAKSPEARE.

THE WAY TO BE HAPPY.

A hermit there was, who lived in a grot,
And the way to be happy they said he had got.
As I wanted to learn it, I went to his cell;
And this answer he gave, when I asked him to tell:
"'T is being, and doing, and having, that make
All the pleasures and pains of which mortals partake:
To *be* what God pleases, to *do* a man's best,
And to *have* a good heart, is the way to be blest."

PERILS OF THE SEA.

The brave ship lay at anchor in the harbor. Her yards were unbraced, and her sails hung loosely against the mast, for the day was calm and lovely. Her port-holes were unclosed, and her guns showed their dark mouths in a fearful row. That was the last time I saw the good ship Terrible. She sailed the next day for China, and was never heard of more.

What was the fate of that noble vessel and her gal'lant crew? Alas! we can only guess. Overtaken by some dreadful storm, did she founder and sink? Or, was she borne against some iceberg that toppled and fell upon her deck, carrying ruin and dismay? Or, did she take fire, and burn to the water's edge? It is conjecture all!

Many are the perils of the poor sailor. Do we ever think how much we owe him? Live comfortably we can not, — live at all, perhaps, we can not, — without seamen will expose themselves for us, risk themselves for us, and, alas! often, very often, drown — drown in our service — drown and leave widows and orphans destitute.

To beg with me, to plead with me, for these destitute ones,

there comes from many a place where seamen have died a call, a prayer, a beseeching voice; — a cry from the coast of Guinea, where there is fever evermore; a cry from Arctic seas, where icebergs are death; a cry from coral reefs, that ships are wrecked on horribly; a cry from mid ocean, where many a sailor drops into a sudden grave! They ask your help, your charity for the widows and orphans of those who have gone down to the sea — have gone down to the sea in ships.

THE MISER AND THE MOUSE.

A MISER, traversing his house,
Espied, unusual there, a mouse,
And thus his uninvited guest,
Briskly inquisitive, addressed:
"Tell me, my dear, to what cause *is* it
I owe this unexpected visit?"
The mouse her host obliquely eyed,
And, smiling, pleasantly replied,
"Fear not, good fellow, for your hoard!
I come to *lodge*, and not to *board*!"

TRANSLATED FROM THE GREEK BY COWPER.

LOVE OF COUNTRY.

BREATHES there the man with soul so dead,
Who never to himself hath said,
This is my own — my native land?
Whose heart hath ne'er within him burned,
As home his footsteps he hath turned
From wandering on a foreign strand?
If such there breathe, go, mark him well:
For him no minstrel raptures swell.

High though his titles, proud his name,
Boundless his wealth as wish can claim —
Despite those titles, power, and pelf,
The wretch, concentered all in self,
Living, shall forfeit fair renown,
And, doubly dying, shall go down
To the vile dust from whence he sprung,
Unwept, unhonored, and unsung!

SIR WALTER SCOTT.

THE CALL OF SAMUEL.

1 Sam. 3 : 1—10.

In Israel's fane, by silent night,
The lamp of God was burning bright;
And there, by viewless angels kept,
Samuel, the child, securely slept.

A voice unknown the stillness broke:
"Samuel!" it called, and thrice it spoke.
He rose; he asked whence came the word; —
From Eli? — No; it was the Lord.

Thus early called to serve his God,
In paths of righteousness he trod;
Prophetic visions fired his breast,
And all the chosen tribes were blessed.

Speak, Lord! and, from our earliest days,
Incline our hearts to love thy ways.
Thy wakening voice hath reached our ear;
Speak, Lord, to us; thy servants hear.

CAWOOD.

CÆSAR'S PASSAGE OF THE RUBICON.

A GENTLEMAN, Mr. President, speaking of Cæsar's benevolent disposition, and of the reluctance with which he entered into the civil war, observes, "How long did he pause upon the brink of the Rubicon!" — How came he to the brink of that river? How dared he cross it? Shall private men respect the boundaries of private property, and shall a man pay no respect to the boundaries of his country's rights? How dared he cross that river? — O! but he paused upon the brink. He should have perished on the brink, ere* he had crossed it!

Why did he pause? — Why does a man's heart palpitate when he is on the point of committing an unlawful deed? Why does the very murderer, his victim sleeping before him, and his glaring eye taking the measure of the blow, strike wide of the mortal part? — Because of conscience! 'T was that made Cæsar pause upon the brink of the Rubicon! — Compassion! What compassion? — The compassion of an assassin, that feels a momentary shudder, as his weapon begins to cut!

Cæsar paused upon the brink of the Rubicon! What was the Rubicon? — The boundary of Cæsar's province. From what did it separate his province? — From his country. Was that country a desert? — No; it was cultivated and fertile, rich and populous! Its sons were men of genius, spirit, and generosity! Its daughters were lovely, susceptible, and chaste! Friendship was its inhabitant! Love was its inhabitant! Domestic affection was its inhabitant! Liberty was its inhabitant! All bounded by the stream of the Rubicon!

What was Cæsar, that stood upon the brink of that stream? — A traitor, bringing war and pestilence into the heart of that country! No wonder that he paused: — no wonder if, his imagination wrought upon by his conscience, he had beheld

* Pronounce *ere*, meaning *before*, like *air*.

blood instead of water, and heard groans instead of murmurs! No wonder if some gorgon horror had turned him into stone upon the spot! But, no! he cried, "The die is cast!" He plunged! he crossed! and Rome was free no more! J. S. KNOWLES.

CASABIANCA.

Young Casabianca, a boy about thirteen years old, son to the Admiral of the Orient, remained at his post in the battle of the Nile, after the ship had taken fire, and all the guns had been abandoned, and perished in the explosion of the vessel, when the flames had reached the powder.

THE boy stood on the burning deck,
Whence all but he had fled;
The flame that lit the battle's wreck
Shone round him o'er the dead.

Yet beautiful and bright he stood,
As born to rule the storm, —
A creature of heroic blood,
A proud, though childlike form.

The flames rolled on — he would not go,
Without his father's word;
That father, faint in death below,
His voice no longer heard.

He called aloud: — "Say, father, say,
If yet my task is done!"
He knew not that the chieftain lay
Unconscious of his son.

"Speak, father!" once again he cried,
"If I may yet be gone!
And ——" But the booming shots replied,
And fast the flames rolled on.

Upon his brow he felt their breath,
  And in his waving hair;
And looked from that lone post of death,
  In still, yet brave despair: —

And shouted but once more aloud,
  "My father! must I stay?"
While o'er him fast, through sail and shroud,
  The wreathing fires made way.

They wrapt the ship in splendor wild,
  They caught the flag on high,
And streamed above the gallant child,
  Like banners in the sky.

There came a burst of thunder sound —
  The boy — O! where was he?
Ask of the winds that far around
  With fragments strewed the sea, —

With mast, and helm, and pennon fair,
  That well had borne their part! —
But the noblest thing which perished there
  Was that young, faithful heart!

MRS. HEMANS.

A ROMAN OFFICER TO HIS SOLDIERS.

SOLDIERS! We are surrounded on all sides by the enemy, and we must do one of two things, — surrender or die, perish or survive in slavery. You, I know, will not hesitate about the choice; but it is not enough to perish — we must perish nobly. The coward may resign himself to be consumed by famine; he may linger in misery, and wait, in a dispirited condition, for the friendly hand of death.

But we, who have been schooled and educated in the field of battle, — we, who are Romans, — we are not now to learn the proper use of our arms; we know how to carve for ourselves an honorable death. Yes, let us die, but not inglorious and unrevenged; let us die covered with the blood of our enemies, that our fall, instead of raising the smile of malicious exultation, may give them cause to mourn over the victory that undoes us. Can we wish to loiter a while longer in life, when we know that a very few years more must bring us to our graves? The limits of human life can not be enlarged by nature; but glory can extend them, and give a second life. Be our resolve, then, this: to perish rather than surrender — to die as men rather than to live as slaves. MARMONTEL.

THE SEASONS.

1*st Voice.* WHEN Spring comes with suns and showers,
What gives beauty to the bowers?
2*d Voice.* Buds and flowers.

1*st V.* When the glowing Summer 's born,
What pours Nature from her horn?
2*nd V.* Hay and corn.

1*st V.* When mild suns in Autumn shine,
Then, O Earth, what gifts are thine?
2*nd V.* Fruit and wine.

1*st V.* When gray Winter comes, what glow
Makes the round earth sparkle so?
2*nd V.* Ice and snow.

1*st V.* Hay and corn, and buds and flowers,
Snow and ice, and fruit and wine;
Spring and Summer, Fall and Winter,

With their suns, and sleets, and showers.
Bring in turn these gifts divine.

2nd V. Spring blows, Summer glows,
Autumn reaps, Winter keeps.
Spring prepares, Summer provides,
Autumn hoards, Winter hides.

Both. Come, then, friends, their praises sound;
Spring and Summer, Autumn, Winter,
Summer, Autumn, Winter, Spring,
As they run their yearly round,
Each in turn with gladness sing!
Time drops blessings as he flies,
Time makes ripe, and Time makes wise.

FROM THE GERMAN.

THE FIR-TREE AND THE THORN. — A Fable.

The lowly and contented state
Is farthest from the wounds of fate.

A Fir, upon a humble Thorn,
From his high top looked down with scorn.
"For loftiest fanes we grow," he said;
"Of us the tallest masts are made;
While thou, poor Bramble, canst produce
Nothing of ornament or use."
"Great tree," the modest Thorn replied,
"When the sharp ax shall pierce your side,
In vain you then may wish to be
Unsought-for and unknown like me."

THE LIFE OF A BIRD.

How pleasant the life of a bird must be,
Skimming about on the breezy sea,
Cresting the billows like silvery foam,
And then wheeling away to its cliff-built home!
What joy it must be to sail, upborne
By a strong free wing, through the rosy morn,
To meet the young sun face to face,
And pierce like a shaft the boundless space!

How pleasant the life of a bird must be!
Wherever it listeth, there to flee;
To go, when a joyful fancy calls,
Dashing adown 'mong the waterfalls,
Then wheeling about with its mates at play,
Above and below, and among the spray,
Hither and thither, with screams as wild
As the laughing mirth of a rosy child!

What joy it must be, like a living breeze,
To flutter about 'mong the flowering trees;
Lightly to soar, and to see beneath
The wastes of the blossoming purple heath,

And the yellow furze, like fields of gold,
That gladden some fairy regions old! —
On mountain tops, on the billowy sea,
On the leafy stems of the forest tree,
How pleasant the life of a bird must be!

MARY HOWITT.

THE FOOT-BALL ORATORS.

I.

Champion of the Blues.

GENTLEMEN of our side! Undaunted Blues! The moment is at hand when you must either exult as victors, or be laid low in the dust as vanquished. The great annual foot-ball battle between the honorable Blues and the detested Greens is now to come off. What can I say to add to the generous ardor that fires your minds? If we allow ourselves to be beaten, — beaten by the Greens, the pusillanimous Greens, — where and how shall we hide our diminished heads? For us no minstrel raptures will swell. For us no laurel wreath will be woven. We shall go down to the base dust from which we sprung — unwept, unhonored, and unsung.

But, if we prevail, — and when I look on your glowing faces and flashing eyes, I feel that we *shall* prevail; I know that there is no such word as *fail;* — *if* we prevail, did I say? no! *when* we prevail — what glory will be ours! We shall draw a freer breath; we shall tread with a prouder step; we shall feel that we, too, are associated with the Alexanders and the Cæsars, with the Fredericks and the Napoleons, of history.

Does any dastard pretend to say that fame is but an empty name? or that, if there is any glory, it will attach to me, your leader, and not to the common soldier? Base and unworthy insinuation! Here I resign it all freely to you in advance. Let me lead you to victory, and the spoils and the glory may be his who can get them.

Intrepid sons of your country! Bravest of brave men! True Blues! Throw off your jackets! Tighten your belts! Don't waste your kicks, but wait till you are sure the ball is before you. Now stand at ease, and wait for the word of command.

II.

Champion of the Greens.

Comrades! Companions in arms! Illustrious Greens! Our strength lies more in deeds than words. If we can not brag as well as the gentlemen of the other side, we may, perhaps, show them that we can *kick* as well, when the time comes. If we do not win this match, it will not be for want of superior wind, tougher shins, and stronger sinews. Our training, too, has been better. We have kept more in the open air — eaten less and exercised more. We are better organized. There stands the larger mob; here stands the stronger army.

Let us meet them like true Americans, and charge home! Do not shrink from the thickest of the scuffle when the ball is to be rescued. Press where ye see my green ribbon flutter amid the ranks of war! Let no man fear for his shins. Let the enemy find, to their sorrow, whose shins are the more tender. Let the abhorred Blues — the tongue-valiant, forcible-feeble Blues — be sent limping from the field home to their anxious mothers, who probably do not know that they are out.

But I will not waste time in words. The hour strikes. The ball is in the air. Now every man to his post! Now, guards! up and at them! Charge! SPENCER.

A CHARACTER.

WHO traced these lines, upon the world was thrown,
Alike "to fortune and to fame unknown;"
So very poor, his only store was health;
So very rich, he envied no man's wealth;
So very proud, he owed a debt to none;
So very bold, he never feared a dun,.
So very brave, he kissed no tyrant's rod;
So very cowardly, he feared his God;
So idle, that he loved to muse and dream;
So selfish, that he loved his self-esteem;
So tame, he swore not when dispute grew loudest;
So fierce, he brooked no insult from the proudest;
So hot, a slanderer well-nigh drove him mad;
So cold, he formed no friendships with the bad;
So timid, that he dared not be a slave;
So stubborn, that he would not be a knave;
So ignorant of life, he hoped and feared
As fortune's varying sky o'ercast or cleared;
So ignorant of law, he knew no better
Than to prefer the spirit to the letter;
So poor a drudge, he earned his daily bread;
So odd, he thanked the Giver as he fed;
So loyal, he abused nor church nor state;
So rancorous, a villain moved his hate;
So insolent, a fool provoked his scorn;
So foolish, that he pitied the forlorn;
So old, at last, he grieved that youth had wings
So young, even then he loved all lovely things;
So childish, that his heart could burn and bleed;
And "whom it loved, loved tenderly indeed!"

J. G. GRANT.

PRECEPTS.

First worship God: he that forgets to pray
Bids not himself good-morrow nor good-day;
Let thy first labor be, to purge thy sin,
And serve Him first whence all things did begin.

Honor thy parents to prolong thine end:
With them, though for a truth, do not contend;
Whoever makes his father's heart to bleed
May have a child that will avenge the deed.

Think that is just: 't is not enough to *do*,
Unless thy very *thoughts* are upright too.
Defend the truth; for that who will not die,
A coward is, and gives himself the lie.

Take well whate'er shall chance; though bad it be,
Take it for good, and 't will be good to thee.
First think; and, if thy thoughts approve thy will,
Then speak; and after that thy speech fulfill.

THOMAS RANDOLPH.

RIENZI TO THE ROMANS.

I, that speak to you, —
I had a brother once, — a gracious boy,
Full of all gentleness, of calmest hope,
Of sweet and quiet joy; there was the look
Of heaven upon his face, which limners give
To the beloved disciple. How I loved
That gracious boy! Younger by fifteen years,
Brother at once and son! He left my side,
A summer bloom on his fair cheeks, a smile
Parting his innocent lips. In one short hour,

The pretty, harmless boy was slain! I saw
The corse, the mangled corse, and then I cried
For vengeance! Rouse, ye Romans! rouse, ye slaves!
Have ye brave sons?—Look, in the next fierce brawl,
To see them die! Have ye daughters fair?—Look
To see them live, torn from your arms, distained,
Dishonored! and, if ye dare call for justice,
Be answered by the lash! Yet this is Rome,
That sat on her seven hills, and, from her throne
Of beauty, ruled the world! Yet we are Romans!
Why, in that elder day, to be a Roman
Was greater than a king! — And once again, —
Hear me, ye walls, that echoed to the tread
Of either Brutus! — once again I swear,
The eternal city shall be free! her sons
Shall walk with princes! MISS MITFORD.

THE APPEAL OF THE CHILDREN.

GIVE us light amid our darkness;
Let us know the good from ill;
Hate us not for all our blindness;
Love us, lead us, show us kindness —
You can make us what you will.

We are willing, we are ready;
We would learn, if you would teach:
We have hearts that yearn towards duty;
We have minds alive to beauty;
Souls that any heights can reach!

Raise us by your Christian knowledge:
Consecrate to man our powers;

Let us take our proper station;
We, the rising generation,
Let us stamp the age as ours!

We shall be what you will make us: —
Make us wise, and make us good!
Make us strong for time of trial;
Teach us temperance, self-denial,
Patience, kindness, fortitude!

Look into our childish faces;
See ye not our willing hearts?
Only love us — only lead us;
Only let us know you need us,
And we all will do our parts.

MARY HOWITT.

THE SOLDIER'S DREAM.

Our bugles sang truce — for the night-cloud had lowered,
And the sentinel stars set their watch in the sky;
And thousands had sunk on the ground overpowered,
The weary to sleep, and the wounded to die.

When reposing that night on my pallet of straw,
By the wolf-scaring fagot that guarded the slain,
At the dead of the night a sweet vision I saw,
And thrice ere the morning I dreamed it again.

Methought from the battle-field's dreadful array
Far, far I had roamed on a desolate track;
'T was autumn — and sunshine arose on the way
To the home of my fathers, that welcomed me back.

I flew to the pleasant fields, traversed so oft
In life's morning march, when my bosom was young;

I heard my own mountain-goats bleating aloft,
  And knew the sweet strain that the corn-reapers sung.

Then pledged we the wine-cup, and fondly I swore
  From my home and my weeping friends never to part;
My little ones kissed me a thousand times o'er,
  And my wife sobbed aloud in her fullness of heart.

"Stay, stay with us — rest, thou art weary and worn;"
  And fain was their war-broken soldier to stay;
But sorrow returned with the dawning of morn,
  And the voice in my dreaming ear melted away.

CAMPBELL.

GOOD ADVICE.

Ye who would save your features flŏrid,
Līthe limbs, bright eyes, unwrinkled forehead,
From Age's devastation horrid,
    Adopt this plan:
'T will make, in climate cold or torrid,
    A hale old man.

Avoid in youth luxurious diet;
Restrain the passions' lawless riot;
Devoted to domestic quiet,
    Be wisely gay;
So shall ye, spite of Age's fiat,
    Resist decay.

Seek not in Mammon's worship pleasure,
But find a far superior treasure
In books, friends, music, polished leisure:
    The mind, not sense,
Make the sole scale by which ye measure
    Your opulence.

This is the solace, this the science, —
With trust in God, life's best appliance, —
That disappoints not man's reliance,
Whate'er his state;
But challenges, with calm defiance,
Time, fortune, fate. HORACE SMITH.

THE REFORMED LAP-DOG.

A RICH old lady's pampered dog
Lay on his cushion like a log. —
Sick with indulgences and ease,
And cross, and difficult to please,
So fat and lazy was he grown,
Scarce could he waddle up and down.

Minions who cease to be protected
May soon expect to be neglected.
Old madam died; and then poor Tray
Was cuffed and kicked, and sent away
A laborer in the neighborhood,
To whom the lady had been good,
Received him in his little shed;
Where, hardly lodged, and scantly fed,
Air, exercise, and temperate board,
Tray's health and spirits soon restored.
Contented in a cottage more
Than with his luxuries before,
His playful tricks and ready glee
Delighted all the family.

O, parents! heed the lap-dog's fate,
And check, before it is too late,

The hand that to the young would give
The means luxuriously to live.
Ease, indolence, and dainty fare,
Their health and vigor must impair.
The tempting food, the pampered state,
Must soon a thousand ills create.
To make us what we ought to be,
No school is like adversity.

THE TRUE LIFE.

If we would judge of the *rate* at which we are living, we are to look not at the growth or the decay of the frame, the tightening or slackening of the sinews, but at the emotions that play most freely through our hearts, and the actions we achieve. Count not your birth-days, but the number of hearts you have blessed, and the holy impulses you have set in motion, if you would know how old you are!

> "Life 's more than breath and the quick round of blood;
> 'T is a great spirit and a busy heart.
> We live in deeds, not years; in thoughts, not breaths;
> In feelings, not in figures on a dial."

The memorial of goodness is everlasting. Whoever bears a working hand and a large love through the world, shall make eternal room for himself in its memory. Whoever speaks fruitful words, so laden with truth that they plant themselves in the hearts of other men with an immovable lodgment, and strike root there, shall realize the fulfillment of the inarticulate prophecy within him, and shall not wholly die, even out of this scene of his present habitation.

HUNTINGTON.

COQUETRY AND SINCERITY.

WHAT 's a coquet? Since none are by
To hear my frank and plain reply,
I'll tell you, that she is by nature
A forward, trifling, heartless creature;
A common glass, all forms reflecting,
Preferring none, and none rejecting;
A gambler who invites your stakes
While in false coin her own she makes;
Who aims at common admiration
By practicing dissimulation;
Who, loving her sweet self alone,
Would win all hearts, and keep her own.

How differently does Chloë charm!
No treachery hers, no false alarm!
With native unaffected grace,
The light of truth is on her face:
Her teeth of pearl, and lips of rose,
Only a smile sincere compose.
For honest love and friendship made,
She scorns the trifler's paltry trade.

The few she loves intent to please,
None other can disturb her ease;
On no new victories she dreams,
But *is* the lovely thing she *seems*.

SUPPOSED SPEECH OF JOHN ADAMS.

Sink or swim, live or die, survive or perish, I give my hand and my heart to this vote. It is true, indeed, that in the beginning we aimed not at independence. But there 's a divinity which shapes our ends. The injustice of England has driven us to arms; and, blinded to her own interest for our good, she has obstinately persisted, till independence is now within our grasp. We have but to reach forth to it, and it is ours. Sir, the war must go on. We must fight it through. And if the war must go on, why put off longer the declaration of independence? That measure will strengthen us. It will give us character abroad.

If we fail, it can be no worse for us. But we shall not fail. The cause will raise up armies; the cause will create navies. The people, the people, if we are true to them, will carry us, and will carry themselves, gloriously, through this struggle. I care not how fickle other people have been found. I know the people of these colonies, and I know that resistance to British aggression is deep and settled in their hearts, and can not be eradicated.

Read this declaration at the head of the army; — every sword will be drawn from its scabbard, and the solemn vow uttered to maintain it, or to perish on the bed of honor. Publish it from the pulpit; — religion will approve it. Send it to the public halls — and the very walls will cry out in its support.

Sir, I know the uncertainty of human affairs; but I see

clearly through this day's business. You and I, indeed, may rue it. We may die, — die colonists; die slaves; die, it may be, ignominiously on the scaffold. But, whatever may be our fate, be assured that this Declaration will stand. We shall make this a glorious, an immortal day. Our children will honor it. They will celebrate it with thanksgiving, with festivity, with bonfires, and illuminations.

Sir, my judgment approves this measure, and my whole heart is in it. All that I have, and all that I am, and all that I hope, in this life, I am now ready here to stake upon it; and I leave off, as I began, that, live or die, survive or perish, I am for the Declaration! It is my living sentiment, and, by the blessing of God, it shall be my dying sentiment, — Independence now, and Independence for ever! WEBSTER.

RISE EARLY.

INSIDIOUS Slōth her object gains
If but a hearing she obtains.

A youth accustomed to sleep late,
And make the breakfast-table wait,
Was asked, "Why lie so long in bed?" —
"I listen to a cause," he said;
"As soon as I unclose my eyes
My better angel bids me rise:
'Up! up!' she says, 'to meet the sun;
Your task of yesterday 's undone;
A thousand fresh delights you miss
In dozing at an hour like this;
You lengthen out the hours of slumber
Beyond what health and nature number:
Arise, if you a man would be!
From these enfeebling toils be free!'

'Lie still,' cries Sloth; 'it is not warm;
An hour's more sleep can do no harm;
You will have time your work to do,
And leisure for amusement too.'" —
Much must be heard on either side,
The question fairly to decide;
And e'er the long debate is o'er,
Time and occasion are no more!
Would you the joy of victory know,
Pause not to parley with the foe:
Play not the sluggard and the dunce, —
Awake! arise! start up at once!

THE BOASTING TRAVELER.

A FELLOW who abroad had been
Told marvels he had done and seen.
"When resident at Rhodes," he said,
"A leap of twenty yards I made
Over a barrier ten feet high;
A dozen witnesses were by."
His hearers at each other wink,
Or by a shrug tell what they think.
"Come on," says one, who near him stood;
"Yon empty ditch and fence of wood
Are, neither, half so high or wide;
Here let the experiment be tried:
Suppose yourself at Rhodes, and we
Your faithful witnesses will be."
The man replied: "Hem! I to-day
Am not quite well," — then stole away.

Avoid the boasting vein, if you
Would not be scorned and laughed at too.

THE CHAMELEON.

Because I may not think like you,
Don't call me foolish or untrue.
So limited is mortal ken,
So blinded are the wisest men, —
Things are so various to the sight, —
Even *you* at times may miss the right;
And even *your* opinion prove
An error time must soon remove.

The question, not long since, arose,
What the chameleon's color was.
A man who had one lately seen
Maintained the creature's hue was green:
Another vehemently said,
Its skin was of a lively red:
To end the contest, they apply
To a third traveler, passing by.
"Sirs, you are neither of you right,"
He cries, — "the animal is white.
To prove it to you, I will show
You one I caught an hour ago." —
The creature from a bag he drew,
When, lo! to their dismay, 't was blue!

A HYMN OF LIBERTY.

God has been bountiful! Garlands of beauty
Grow all around, making gladness a duty;
Shedding their bloom on the pale cheek of slavery,
Holding out plumes for the helmets of bravery;
Voices proclaiming, from field and from wave,
"God has been bountiful — man must be brave!"

Look on this harvest of plenty and promise —
Shall we sleep while the enemy snatches it from us?
Would ye live happily? Fear not nor falter; —
Peace crowns the summit of Liberty's altar.
Would ye win Glory? She knows not the slave;
God has been bountiful — you must be brave!

Come, vow by the bright streams abundantly flowing,
And by the cold hearth-stones where wet weeds are growing,
By the stars, and the earth, and the four winds of heaven,
That the land shall be saved, and its tyrants outdriven!
Do it! and blessings will shelter your grave:
God has been bountiful — will *ye* be brave?

DUBLIN NATION.

THE HIDDEN TREASURE.

WORK, work, my boys, with hand and mind!
Your labors you will fruitful find.

A husbandman, about to die,
Called on his children to come nigh:
"I leave," he said, "a small estate,
But wherewithal to make it great:
For, know a treasure it contains,
If you to search will take the pains." —
He died. The sons dug all the ground,
But there no hidden treasure found:
Yet so productive was the soil,
The crop soon overpaid their toil.
Says one, when they their corn had sold,
"This was the hoard our sire foretold."

THE SKATER'S SONG.

Away, away, o'er the glistening ice,
  Away, away, we go;
On our steel-bound feet we move as fleet
  As deer o'er the Lapland snow.
What though the sharp north winds are out?
  The skater heeds them not;
'Mid the laugh and shout of the joyous rout,
  Grim Winter is forgot.

Let others choose more gentle sports,
  By the side of the parlor fire;
Or 'neath the lamps of the festal hall
  A close, warm air respire:
But as for me — away! away!
  Where the skaters glide and wheel;
Where the pure, fresh gale 't is a joy to inhale,
  And a luxury to feel!

For there we know we are hand in hand
  With that jovial comrade, Health;
Who bringeth a cheer that we find not near
  In revelry, fame, or wealth.

Then let us go when the north winds blow
To the pond by the old bare wood;
And a glow that fire can not bestow
Shall stir and kindle the blood.

THE MAN OF INTEGRITY.

It will not take much time to delineate the character of the man of integrity, as by its nature it is a plain one, and easily understood. He is one who makes it his constant rule to follow the road of duty, according as the word of God and the voice of his conscience point it out to him. He is not guided merely by affections, which may sometimes give the color of virtue to a loose and unstable character.

The upright man is guided by a fixed principle of mind, which determines him to esteem nothing but what is honorable, and to abhor whatever is base or unworthy, in moral conduct. Hence we find him ever the same; at all times the trusty friend, the affectionate relation, the conscientious man of business, the pious worshiper, the public-spirited citizen.

He assumes no borrowed appearance. He seeks no mask to cover him, for he acts no studied part; but he is indeed what he appears to be, full of truth, candor, and humanity. In all his pursuits, he knows no path but the fair and direct one; and would much rather fail of success, than attain it by reproachful means.

He never shows us a smiling countenance, while he meditates evil against us in his heart. He never praises us among our friends, and then joins in traducing us among our enemies. We shall never find one part of his character at variance with another. In his manners, he is simple and unaffected; in all his proceedings, open and consistent. BLAIR.

THE WORDS OF HOPE.

I SAY to thee, do thou repeat
To the first man thou mayest meet,
In lane, highway, or open street, —

That he, and we, and all men, move
Under a canopy of love,
As broad as the blue sky above:

That doubt and trouble, fear and pain,
And anguish, all are shadows vain;
That death itself shall not remain:

That weary deserts we may tread,
A dreary labyrinth we may thread,
Through dark ways under ground be led;

Yet, if we will our Guide obey,
The dreariest path, the darkest way,
Shall issue out in heavenly day; —

And we, on divers shores now cast,
Shall meet, our perilous voyage past,
All in our Father's house, at last!

And ere thou leave him, say thou this
Yet one word more: they only miss
The winning of that final bliss,

Who will not count it true that Love,
Blessing, not cursing, rules above,
And that in it we live and move: —

And one thing further make him know:
That to believe these things are so,
This firm faith never to forego, —

Despite of all which seems at strife
With blessing, all with curses rife, —
That this is blessing, this is life.

THE DEAN OF WESTMINSTER.

HECTOR AND ANDROMACHE.*

And. Too daring prince! — Ah! whither dost thou run?
Ah! too forgetful of thy wife and son!
And think'st thou not how wretched we shall be?
A widow I, a helpless orphan he!
For sure such courage length of life denies;
And thou must fall, thy virtue's sacrifice.

Hec. Andromache! my soul's far better part,
Why with untimely sorrow heaves thy heart?
No hostile hand can antedate my doom,
Till fate condemn me to the silent tomb.

And. Greece in her single heroes strove in vain;
Now hosts oppose thee, and thou must be slain.
No parent now remains my griefs to share,
No father's aid, no mother's tender care;
Yet, while my Hector still survives, I see
My father, mother, brethren, all in thee!
Alas! my parents, brethren, kindred, all
Once more will perish, if my Hector fall!

Hec. My early youth was bred to warlike pains;
My soul impels me to the martial plains.
Still foremost let me stand to guard the throne,
To save my father's honors and my own.

And. That quarter most the skillful Greeks annoy
Where yon wild fig-trees join the wall of Troy:

* Pronounced *An-drom'a-ke.*

Thou from this tower defend the important post;
There Agamem'non points his dreadful host:
Thrice our bold foes the fierce attack have given,
Or led by hopes, or dictated from Heaven.
Let others in the field their arms employ;
But stay my Hector here, and guard his Troy.
Hec. How would the sons of Troy, in arms renowned,
And Troy's proud dames, whose garments sweep the ground,
Attaint the luster of my former name,
Should Hector basely quit the field of fame!
No more — but hasten to thy tasks at home;
There guide the spindle, and direct the loom.

HOMER, TRANSLATED BY POPE.

THE BUTTERFLY'S BALL.

Come, take up your hats, and away let us haste
To the Butterfly's ball and the Grasshopper's feast;
The trumpeter Gadfly has summoned the crew,
And the revels are now only waiting for you.

On the smooth-shaven grass by the side of the wood,
Beneath a broad oak that for ages has stood,
See the children of earth and the tenants of air
For an evening's amusement together repair.

And there came the Beetle, so blind and so black,
Who carried the Emmet, his friend, on his back;
And there was the Gnat, and the Dragonfly too,
With all their relations, green, orange, and blue.

And there came the Moth in his plumage of down,
And Hornet with jacket of yellow and brown,
Who with him the Wasp, his companion, did bring;
But they promised that evening to lay by their sting.

And the sly little Dormouse crept out of his hole,
And led to the feast his blind brother, the Mole;
And the Snail, with his horns peeping out from his shell,
Came from a great distance, — the length of an ell.

A mushroom their table, and on it was laid
A water-dock leaf, which a table-cloth made;
The viands were various, to suit each one's taste,
And the Bee brought his honey to crown the repast.

There, close on his haunches, so solemn and wise,
The Frog from a corner looked up to the skies;
And the Squirrel, well pleased such diversion to see,
Sat cracking his nuts overhead in a tree.

Then out came the Spider, with fingers so fine,
To show his dexterity on the tight line;
From one branch to another his cobwebs he slung,
Then as quick as an arrow he darted along.

But just in the middle, — O! shocking to tell! —
From his rope in an instant poor Harlequin fell;
Yet he touched not the ground, but with talons outspread
Hung suspended in air at the end of a thread.

Then a Grasshopper came with a jerk and a spring, —
Very long was his leg, though but short was his wing:
He took but three leaps and was soon out of sight,
Then chirped his own praises the rest of the night.

With step so majestic the Snail did advance,
And promised the gazers a minuet to dance;
But they all laughed so loud that he pulled in his head,
And went to his own little chamber to bed.

Then, as evening gave way to the shadows of night,
Their watchman, the Glowworm, came out with his light;
Then home let us hasten while yet we can see,
For no watchman is waiting for you or for me.

ROSCOE.

SPARTACUS TO HIS FELLOW-GLADIATORS.

FELLOW-GLAD′IATORS! Why droop we thus, and chafe in sullen desperation? We have strong limbs; we have sharp swords. Let us turn them no longer against one another, for Rome's inhuman pastime:—let us turn them against our tyrants! What though they are many, and we are few? Is not one of us a match for a dozen of these effeminate lords? What though they are rich, and we are poor? Have we not an inheritance of wrongs too vast, almost, to be reckoned?

Listen, brothers! The city is wrapt in sleep. The guards that would oppose us may be easily overpowered, and their weapons seized. Thus doubly armed, we may make our way into the open country, and by sunrise be able to defy our masters.—Masters, did I say? Are we not grown men, and, by the law of nature, our own masters only?

O Liberty! blessing which they only who have lost can duly prize—do we indeed behold thee in the distance, beckoning us to thy embrace? Yes, it is she, my brethren! And what must we do to reach her? This merely—*dare!* In that one word lies the secret—*dare!*

Rise, then, ye victims of Roman cruelty and pride! Resolve to be slaves no longer! Are we not armed? At least, we can die like men, fighting for our freedom, hewing down our oppressors,—selling our lives at a dear price, not cheaply on the shambles of the a-re′na. Up, then, and on! Victory is to the brave. Adventures are to the adventurous. Follow me. The first step, remember, is—*dare!* OSBORNE.

THE WAR-HORSE.

Hast thou given the horse strength? hast thou clothed his neck with thunder?

Canst thou make him afraid as a grasshopper? The glory of his nostrils is terrible.

He paweth in the valley, and rejoiceth in his strength: he goeth on to meet the armed men.

He mocketh at fear, and is not affrighted; neither turneth he back from the sword.

The quiver rattleth against him, the glittering spear and the shield.

He swalloweth the ground with fierceness and rage: neither believeth he that it is the sound of the trumpet.

He saith among the trumpets, Ha, ha! and he smelleth the battle afar off, the thunder of the captains, and the shouting. JOB.

THE CHILD'S FIRST GRIEF.

"O! CALL my brother back to me! —
I can not play alone!
The summer comes with flower and bee -
Where is my brother gone?

"The butterfly is glancing bright
Across the sunbeam's track:
I care not now to chase its flight —
O, call my brother back!

"The flowers run wild — the flowers we sowed
Around our garden tree;
Our vine is drooping with its load —
O, call him back to me!"

"He would not hear my voice, fair child!
He may not come to thee;
The face that once like spring-time smiled
On earth no more thou 'lt see.

"The rose's brief, bright life of joy,
Such unto him was given:
Go, — thou must play alone, my boy!
Thy brother is in heaven."

"And has he left his birds and flowers?
And must I call in vain?
And through the long, long summer hours,
Will he not come again?

"And by the brook, and in the glade,
Are all our wanderings o'er?
O! while my brother with me played,
Would I had loved him more!"

MRS. HEMANS.

THE FOLLY OF PRIDE.

TAKE some quiet, sober moment of life, and add together the two ideas of pride and of man; behold him, a creature of a span high, stalking through infinite space, in all the grandeur of littleness. Perched on a little speck of the universe, every wind of heaven strikes into his blood the coldness of death; his soul fleets from his body, like melody from the string; day and night, as dust on the wheel, he is rolled along the heavens, through a labyrinth of worlds, and all the systems and creations of God are flaming above and beneath.

Is this a creature to revel in his greatness? Is this a creature to make to himself a crown of glory; to deny his own flesh and blood; and to mock at his fellow, sprung from that dust to which they both will soon return? Does the proud man not err? Does he not suffer? Does he not die? When he reasons, is he never stopped by difficulties? When he acts, is he never tempted by pleasures? When he lives, is he free from pain? When he dies, can he escape from the common grave? Pride is not the heritage of man; humility should dwell with frailty, and atone for ignorance, error, and imperfection. SIDNEY SMITH.

ON EMPLOYING INDIANS AGAINST THE AMERICANS.

MY LORDS, this barbarous measure has been defended, not only on the principles of policy and necessity, but also on those of morality; "for it is perfectly allowable," says Lord Suffolk, "to use all the means which God and nature have put into our hands." I am astonished, shocked, to hear such principles confessed; to hear them avowed in this house, or in this country!

My lords, I did not intend to trespass again on your attention; but I can not repress my indignation; — I feel myself impelled to speak. My lords, we are called upon as members of this house, as men, as Christian men, to protest against such notions. "That God and nature have put into our hands!" — I know not what ideas that noble lord may entertain of God and nature; but I know that such abominable principles are equally abhorrent to religion and humanity. What! attribute the sacred sanction of God and nature to the massacres of the Indian scalping-knife! to the cannibal savage, torturing, murdering, devouring, — literally, my lords, devouring the mangled victims of his barbarous battles! Such horrible notions shock every precept of religion, revealed or natural, and every generous feeling of humanity; and, my lords, they shock every sentiment of honor.

These abominable principles, and this more abominable avowal of them, demand the most decisive indignation! I call upon that right reverend and this most learnëd bench, to vindicate the religion of their God, to support the justice of their country. I call upon the bishops to interpose the unsullied sanctity of their lawn, — upon the judges, to interpose the purity of their ermine, to save us from this pollution. I call upon the honor of your lordships, to reverence the dignity of your ancestors, and to maintain your own. I call upon the spirit and humanity of my country, to vindicate the national character. I invoke the genius of the constitution. I solemnly call upon your lordships, and upon every order of men in the state, to stamp upon this infamous procedure the indelible stigma of the public abhorrence!

EARL OF CHATHAM.

DELAY NOT.

"To-morrow, not to-day, I'll do it!"
'T is thus the idle learn to rue it: —
"To-morrow I will strive anew!

To-morrow, no more dissipation!
To-morrow, serious application!
  To-morrow, this and that I 'll do."

And wherefore not *to-day?* To-morrow
Will also be for thee too narrow:
  To every day its task assign!
What 's done, we know is *done* for ever;
But what to-morrow granteth, never
  Can be foreseen by wit of thine.

On! on! or thou wilt be retreating;
For flesh is weak, and time is fleeting:
  Advance, or thou wilt backward go!
What we have *now*, is in our power,—
The present good, the present hour,—
  The future, who can claim or know?

Each day, in base inaction fleeing,
Is, in the volume of thy being,
  A page unwritten, blank, and void:
O! write on its unsullied pages
Deeds to be read by coming ages:
  Be every day alike employed!

THE SPIDER AND THE FLY.

"Will you walk into my parlor?" said the spider to the fly;
"'T is the prettiest little parlor that ever you did spy;
The way into the parlor is up a winding stair,
And I have many a curious thing to show when you are there!"
"O, no, no!" said the little fly; "to ask me is in vain,
For who goes up your winding stair can ne'er come down again."

"I 'm sure you must be weary, dear, with soaring up so high;
Will you rest upon my little bed?" said the spider to the fly:

"There are pretty curtains drawn around, the sheets are fine and thin,
And if you like to rest a while, I 'll snugly tuck you in."
"O, no, no," said the little fly; "for I 've often heard it said,
They never, never wake again, who sleep upon your bed."

Said the cunning spider to the fly, "Dear friend, what can I do
To prove the warm affection I 've always felt for you?
I have, within my pantry, good store of all that 's nice;
I 'm sure you 're very welcome, — will you please to take a slice?"
"O, no, no," said the little fly; "kind sir, that can not be;
I 've heard what 's in your pantry, and I do not wish to see."

"Sweet creature," said the spider, "you 're witty and you 're wise;
How handsome are your gaudy wings, how brilliant are your eyes
I have a little looking-glass upon my parlor shelf:
If you 'll step in one moment, dear, you shall behold yourself."
"I thank you, gentle sir," she said, "for what you 're pleased to say,
And, bidding you good-morrow now, I 'll call another day."

The spider turned him round about, and went into his den,
For well he knew the silly fly would soon come back again.
So he wove a subtle web in a little corner sly,
And set his table ready to dine upon the fly,
Then he came out to his door again, and merrily did sing,
"Come hither, hither, pretty fly, with the pearl and silver wing;
Your robes are green and purple, there 's a crest upon your head;
Your eyes are like the diamond bright, but mine are dull as lead."

Alas! alas! how very soon this silly little fly,
Hearing his wily, flattering words, came slowly flitting by!
With buzzing wings she hung aloft, then near and nearer drew,
Thinking only of her brilliant eyes, and green and purple hue;
Thinking only of her crested head, poor foolish thing! at last
Up jumped the cunning spider, and fiercely held her fast.

He dragged her up his winding stair, into his dismal den,
Within his little parlor, — but she ne'er came out again!
And now, my dear young pupils, who may this story read,
To idle, silly, flattering words, I pray you give no heed;
Unto an evil counselor close heart, and ear, and eye,
And take a lesson from this tale of the spider and the fly.

MARY HOWITT.

THE USE OF FLOWERS.

God might have made the earth bring forth
  Enough for great and small, —
The oak-tree and the cedar-tree, —
  Without a flower at all.

Then, wherefore, wherefore were they made,
  All dyed with rainbow light,
All fashioned with supremest grace,
  Upspringing day and night, —

Springing in valleys green and low,
  And on the mountains high,
And in the silent wilderness,
  Where no man passes by?

Our outward life requires them not, —
  Then wherefore had they birth?
To minister delight to man!
  To beautify the earth!

To comfort man, — to whisper hope,
  Whene'er his faith is dim!
For He who careth for the flower
  Will much more care for *him*.

MARY HOWITT.

THE ALARM.

Up the hillside, down the glen,
Rouse the sleeping citizen,
Summon out the might of men!

Like a lion crouching low,
Like a night-storm rising slow,
Like the tread of unseen foe, —

It is coming — it is nigh!
Stand your homes and altars by!
On your own free hearthstones die!

Clang the bells in all your spires! —
On the gray hills of your sires
Fling to heaven your signal-fires!

O! for God and duty stand,
Heart to heart, and hand to hand,
Round the old graves of your land!

Whoso shrinks and falters now,
Whoso to the yoke would bow,
Brand the craven on his brow! WHITTIER.

A WINTER SERMON.

Thou dwellest in a warm and cheerful home,
Thy roof in vain the winter tempest lashes;
While houseless wretches round thy mansion roam,
On whose unsheltered heads the torrent plashes.

Thy board is loaded with the richest meats,
O'er which thine eyes in sated languor wander,
Many might live on what thy mastiff eats,
Or feast on fragments which thy servants squander.

Thy limbs are muffled from the piercing blast,
  When from thy fireside corner thou dost sally;
Many have scarce a rag about them cast,
  With which the frosty breezes toy and dally.

Thou hast soft smiles to greet thy kiss of love,
  When thy light step resounds within the portal;
Some have no friends save Him who dwells above,
  No sweet communion with a fellow-mortal.

Thou sleepest soundly on thy costly bed,
  Lulled by the power of luxuries unnumbered;
Some pillow on a stone an aching head,
  Never again to wake when they have slumbered.

Then think of those, who, formed of kindred clay,
  Depend upon the doles thy bounty scatters;
And God will hear them for thy welfare pray —
  They are His children, though in rags and tatters.

HOUSEHOLD WORDS.

EDUCATION.

On a cold morning, early in spring, I observed an old gardener busy among the bare boughs of his fruit-trees. He plucked a small twig, opened the hard, scaly bud with his pen-knife, and seemed quite engrossed with what appeared to me a very insignificant object. As I knew the gentleman to be no trifler, I began to feel curious to know what he was about; so, as the quickest way to come at the matter, I ventured the question direct: "Pardon me, Uncle Jerry, but what in the world are you searching for in that ill-looking little bud?" The old man smiled, and replied: "A future harvest. There will be plenty of peaches next September, if the frosts hold off." — "I should like to see the proof of so confident a prophecy," said I.

He opened another bud, and showed me what he called the flower-bud; the germ of the future fruit being distinctly visible, though so minute as only to be seen on close inspection. "Sure enough," I said to myself; "here are all the rudiments of the future peach wrapped up and concealed in that diminutive bud." The incident was suggestive, and led to some reflections. Such, thought I, is the *mind* of the *child!* It contains within itself all the germs of its future life, wrapped, concealed, and shielded, in the bud of infancy. What is the proper business of education? What, but the most perfect development of the mind? H. VAIL.

THANKSGIVING HYMN.

Father of earth and heaven,
  Whose arm upholds creation,
To Thee we raise the voice of praise,
  And bend in adoration.

We praise the power that made us;
  We praise the love that blesses;
While every day that rolls away
  Thy gracious care confesses.

Life is from Thee, blest Father;
  From Thee all breathing spirits;
And Thou dost give to all that live
  The bliss that each inherits.

Day, night, and rolling seasons,
  And all that life embraces,
With bliss are crowned, with joy abound,
  And claim our thankful praises.

And when Death's final summons
  From earth's dear scenes shall move us, —
From friends, from foes, from joys, from woes,
  From all that know and love us, —

O, then let hope attend us!
  Thy peace to us be given!
That we may rise above the skies,
  And sing thy praise in heaven!

HORATIUS OFFERS TO DEFEND THE BRIDGE.

THEN outspake brave Horatius,
  The captain of the gate:
"To every man upon this earth
  Death cometh, soon or late;
And how can man die better
  Than facing fearful odds
For the ashes of his fathers
  And the temples of his gods?

"Hew down the bridge, Sir Consul,
  With all the speed ye may;
I, with two more to help me,
  Will hold the foe in play.
In yon strait path a thousand
  May well be stopped by three;
Now, who will stand on either hand,
  And keep the bridge with me?"

Then outspake Spurius Lartius;
  A Ramnian bold was he:
"Lo! I will stand at thy right hand,
  And keep the bridge with thee."

And outspake strong Herminius;
Of Titian blood was he:
"I will abide on thy left side,
And keep the bridge with thee."

"Horatius," quoth the Consul,
"As thou say'st, so let it be!"
And straight against that great array
Forth went the dauntless three.
For Romans in Rome's quarrels
Spared neither land nor gold,
Nor son nor wife, nor limb nor life,
In the brave days of old.

MACAULAY.

LIFE COMPARED TO A RIVER.

River! River! little River!
Bright you sparkle on your way;
O'er the yellow pebbles dancing,
Through the flowers and foliage glancing,
Like a child at play.

River! River! swelling River!
On you rush o'er rough and smooth,
Louder, faster, brawling, leaping
Over rocks, by rose-banks sweeping,
Like impetuous youth.

River! River! brimming River!
Broad and deep and *still* as Time,
Seeming *still*, yet still in motion,
Tending onward to the ocean,
Just like mortal prime.

River! River! rapid River!
  Swifter now you slip away;
Swift and silent as an arrow,
Through a channel dark and narrow,
  Like life's closing day.

River! River! headlong River!
  Down you dash into the sea;
Sea that line hath never sounded,
Sea that voyage hath never rounded,
  Like eternity.

MRS. SOUTHEY.

THE LION AND THE GOATS.

PREFER a safe and humble lot
To luxuries by danger got.

A Lion seeing from below
Goats feeding on a craggy brow,
"Come down," he says; "you here will find
Herbage of a superior kind." —
"We thank you for your royal care,"
Says one, "but like our present fare:
The pasture may not be so good,
But we *in safety* crop our food."

A PRAYER.

FATHER of light and life! thou Good Supreme!
O, teach *me* what is good! teach me *Thyself!*
Save me from folly, vanity, and vice,
From every low pursuit, and feed my soul
With knowledge, conscious peace, and virtue pure —
Sacred, substantial, never-fading bliss!

THOMSON.

NOT AN UNCOMMON COMPLAINT.

Enter JOHN, *followed by a* BEGGAR.

Beggar. FOR the love of mercy, sir, pity a poor boy, and give him alms!

John. Give him alms! Why, you have two stout arms of your own, and look as strong and hearty as a young bear.

Beggar. Ah! sir, it is all a deception. I have a disease about me which I can not well explain to you, but which saps my strength and prevents my working.

John. You a sick man? Let me feel of your pulse. (*Feels of his pulse.*) A good, strong, regular pulse! Why, what 's the matter with you?

Beggar. If you would but give me a little money first, sir, I will tell you all that I know about my complaint.

John. I don't like to encourage beggars; but, since you are an invalid, I will assist you. (*Offering money.*) There 's a quarter of a dollar.

Beggar. Would you take the trouble, sir, to put it in my pocket? You see my arm drops to my side, if I but raise it.

John. Poor fellow! I will make the quarter a half. (*Putting money in the* BEGGAR'S *pocket.*) There! Now let me know all about your troubles.

Beggar. Well, sir, you must know that my father sent me to school, but this complaint of mine prevented my studying. The very sight of a book would bring on a paroxysm. Father then bound me apprentice to a farmer; but, the moment I took a rake or a hoe in hand, I would have a violent attack of this terrible disease, till, sir, I had to give up.

John. Poor, poor fellow! I have but a few cents left, but here they are.

Beggar. Shall I trouble you again, sir? (JOHN *puts them in his pocket.*)

John. You seem to be tired of standing, my poor fellow. Let me hand you a chair. (*Hands him a chair, and helps him to sit down.*)

Beggar. Thank you, sir, thank you; I have felt, all the morning, as if an attack were coming on.

John. How does it come on?

Beggar. Why, sir, I feel all over like a wet rag, and as if I did n't want to move. Sometimes I don't want to drag one foot before the other.

John. Have you taken no medicine?

Beggar. Well, father made me swallow some essence of birch, and tried drenching me with cold water. But nothing would cure me.

John. What do the doctors say?

Beggar. The doctors say that the malady is beyond their reach. One doctor recommended the bastinado.

John. The bastinado? Is that a medicine?

Beggar. Truly, I don't know what it is, sir; but I think it 's an outward application.

John. But what 's the nature of the complaint? What part of your system does it affect in particular?

Beggar. Alas! sir, the disease which afflicts me is far different from what you conceive, and is such as you can not discern; yet it is an evil which has crept over my whole body; it has passed through my veins and marrow, in such a manner that there is no member of my body that is able to work for my daily bread.

John. Is there no name for the disease?

Beggar. O, yes! (*Rising, and yawning*) By some it is called laziness — by others, slōth.

John. (*Trying to strike him with a stick.*) Rascal! Impostor! Give me back my money! I 'll cure you of your disease! (*Chases him about the stage.*) Here is a doctor for you! (*Showing his stick.*) You lazy reprobate! Could not lift your hand to your pocket — eh?

Beggar. O! don't make me run! Don't make me run! (*Exeunt*, JOHN *beating him.*) OSBORNE.

NEW YEAR'S ADDRESS TO CHILDREN.

MY children, 't is the New Year's morn,
And many a wish for you is born,
And many a prayer of spirit true
Breaks from parental lips for you.
The country, too, which gave you birth —
The freest, happiest clime on earth,
To all, to each, with fervor cries,
"Child! for my sake, be good, be wise,
Seek knowledge, and with studious pain
Resolve her priceless gold to gain:
Shun the strong cup, whose poisonous tide
To Ruin's dark abyss doth guide;
And with the sons of Virtue stand,
The bulwark of your native land.
Me would you serve? this day begin
The fear of God, the dread of sin;
Love for instruction's watchful care —
The patient task, the nightly prayer:
So shall you glitter as a gem,
Bound in my brightest diadem."

SPEECH OF A CHOCTAW CHIEF.

BROTHER, my voice is weak; you can scarcely hear me; it is not the shout of a warrior, but the wail of an infant; I have lost it in mourning over the misfortunes of my people. These are their graves, and in those agëd pines you hear the ghosts of the departed. Their ashes are here, and we have been left to protect them. Our warriors are nearly all gone to the far country west; but *here* are our dead. Shall we go, too, and give their bones to the wolves?

Brother, you ask us to leave our country, and you tell us this is the wish of our father, the great white Chief at Washington. Brother, our hearts are full. Twelve winters ago, our chiefs sold our country. Every warrior that you see here was opposed to the treaty. If the dead could have been counted, it would never have been made. But, alas! though they stood around, they could not be seen or heard. Their tears came in the rain-drops, and their voices in the wailing wind. But the pale-faces knew it not, and our land was taken away.

Brother, we do not now complain. The Choctaw suffers, but he never weeps. You have the strong arm, and we can not resist. But the pale-face worships the Great Spirit — so does the red man — and the Great Spirit loves *truth.* When you took our country, you promised us land. There is your promise in the book. Twelve times have the trees dropped down their leaves, and yet we have received no land. Our houses have been taken from us. The white man's plow turns up the bones of our fathers. We dare not kindle our fires; and yet you said we might remain, and you would give us land. Brother, is this *truth?*

You stand in the moccasins of a great chief; you speak the words of a mighty nation. Your talk was long. My people are small; their shadow scarcely reaches to your knees; they are scattered and gone. When I shout, I hear my voice in the depths of the woods, but no answering shout comes back. My words, therefore, are few. I have nothing more to say.

DOMESTIC HARMONY.

Since trifles make the sum of human things,
And half our misery from our foibles springs;
Since life's best joys consist in peace and ease,
And though but few can serve, yet all may please —
O ! let the ungentle spirit learn from hence,
A small unkindness is a great offense.
To spread large bounties though we wish in vain,
Yet all may shun the guilt of giving pain.
To bless mankind with tides of flowing wealth,
With rank to grace them, or to crown with health,
Our little lot denies : but Heaven decrees
To all the gift of ministering to ease; —
The gentle offices of patient love,
Beyond all flattery, and all price above;
The mild forbearance at another's fault;
The taunting word suppressed as soon as thought;
The kind attention — all the peace which springs
From the large aggregate of little things, —
On these small cares of daughter, wife, or friend,
The almost sacred joys of home depend!

A solitary blessing few can find;
Our joys with those we love are intertwined;

And he, whose wakeful tenderness removes
The obstructing thorn which wounds the breast he loves,
Smooths not another's rugged path alone,
But scatters roses to perfume his own!

MRS. H. MORE.

THE BEST WISH.

SAY, my child, what would you do,
If a fairy said to you,
"Bid me only wave my hand,
And before me you shall stand,
Changed in mind, and form, and voice,
To whatever is your choice!"

Soon the child's reply is heard:
"I would be a merry bird,
Playing blithely as I please
Ever 'mid the flowers and trees;
In the sunshine all day long,
And my only task a song!"

"Flowers and sunshine soon will go:
Think, my child, of frost and snow;
When the forest boughs are bare,
Will the bird be singing there?
Pause a while, and then rejoice
That you can not have your choice.

"Rather be a man of worth,
Prompt to do good deeds on earth;
Work with zeal, your task will prove
Easy as the song you love.
They have sunshine, *they* have flowers,
Who look back on well-spent hours!"

T. H. BAYLY.

DAVID'S LAMENT FOR SAUL AND JONATHAN.

The beauty of Israël is slain upon thy high places: how are the mighty fallen!

Tell it not in Gath, publish it not in the streets of Askelon; lest the daughters of the Philistines rejoice, lest the daughters of the uncircumcised triumph.

Ye mountains of Gil-bo'a, let there be no dew, neither let there be rain upon you, nor fields of offerings: for there the shield of the mighty is vilely cast away, the shield of Saul, as though he had not been anointed with oil.

From the blood of the slain, from the fat of the mighty, the bow of Jonathan turned not back, and the sword of Saul returned not empty.

Saul and Jonathan were lovely and pleasant in their lives, and in their death they were not divided; they were swifter than eagles, they were stronger than lions.

Ye daughters of Israël, weep over Saul, who clothed you in scarlet, with other delights, who put on ornaments of gold upon your apparel.

How are the mighty fallen in the midst of the battle! O Jonathan, thou wast slain in thine high places.

I am distressed for thee, my brother Jonathan: very pleasant hast thou been unto me; thy love to me was wonderful, passing the love of women.

How are the mighty fallen, and the weapons of war perished! BIBLE.

LUCY'S LAMB.

Lucy had a little lamb,
  Its fleece was white as snow,
And every where that Lucy went
  The lamb was sure to go.

He followed her to school one day,
  Which was against the rule;
It made the children laugh and play
  To see a lamb at school.

And so the teacher turned him out;
  But still he lingered near,
And in the grass he fed about
  Till Lucy did appear.

To her he ran, and then he laid
  His head upon her arm,
As if to say, "I 'm not afraid —
  You 'll shield me from all harm."

"What makes the lamb love Lucy so?"
  The little children cried.
"O! Lucy loves the lamb, you know,"
  The teacher quick replied.

SONG OF THE MOUNTAIN BOY.

The mountain shepherd-boy am I!
Castles and lakes beneath me lie!
The sun's first rosy beams are mine;
At eve his latest on me shine;
    I am the mountain-boy!

The flowing torrent here has birth;
I drink it fresh from out the earth;
It gushes from its rocky bed, —
I cătch it with my arms outspread!
    I am the mountain-boy!

To me belongs the mountain height;
Around me tempests wing their flight;

From north and south their blasts they call;
My song is heard above them all;
I am the mountain-boy!

Thunder and lightnings under me,
The blue expanse above I see;
I greet the storms with friendly tone:
"O, leave my father's cot alone!
I am the mountain-boy!"

And when the tocsin calls to arms,
And mountain bale-fires spread alarms,
Then I descend and join the throng,
And swing my sword, and sing my song —
I am the mountain-boy!

FROM THE GERMAN OF UHLAND.

THE THREE HOMES.

"Where is thy home?" I asked a child,
Who, in the morning air,
Was twining flowers most sweet and wild
In garlands for her hair.
"My home," the happy heart replied,
And smiled in childish glee,
"Is on the sunny mountain side,
Where soft winds wander free."
O! blessings fall on artless youth,
And all its rosy hours,
When every word is joy and truth,
And treasures live in flowers!

"Where is thy home?" I asked of one
Who bent, with flushing face,
To hear a warrior's tender tone,
In the wild wood's secret place.

She spoke not, but her varying cheek
The tale might well impart;
The home of her young spirit meek
Was in a kindred heart.
Ah! souls that well might soar above,
To earth will fondly cling,
And build their hopes on human love,
That light and fragile thing!

"Where is thy home, thou lonely man?"
I asked a pilgrim gray,
Who came with furrowed brow, and wan,
Slow moving on his way.
He paused, and with a solemn mien
Upturned his holy eyes, —
"The land I seek thou ne'er hast seen;
My home is in the skies!"
O! blest, thrice blest, the heart must be
To whom such thoughts are given,
That walks from worldly fetters free; —
Its only home is heaven!

VIRTUE AND ERROR.

Many there are who of their lot complain;
Many there are who rail at fate in vain;
But on himself weak man should vent his rage, —
Error in youth must lead to gloom in age.

Many there are content in humblest lot;
Many there are, though poor, who murmur not:
Write, then, in gold, on their recording page, —
Virtue in youth must lead to bliss in age.

T. H. BAYLY.

OUR FAVORITE PLACE.

Where the silvery pond is brightest,
Where the lilies grow the whitest,
Where the river meets the sea, —
That 's the place for Frank and me.

Where the dovecot is the neatest,
Where the blackbird sings the sweetest,
Where the nestlings chirp and flee, —
That 's the place for Frank and me.

Where the mowers mow the cleanest,
Where the hay lies thick and greenest,
Where is seen the homeward bee, —
That 's the place for Frank and me.

Where the sunny bank is steepest,
Where the cooling shade is deepest,
Where the ripened nuts fall free, —
That 's the place for Frank and me.

WORK AND PLAY.

Work while you work, play while you play:
That is the way to be cheerful and gay.

All that you do, do with your might;
Things done by halves are never done right.

One at a time, and that done well,
Is a good rule, as I can tell.

Moments are useless, trifled away;
Work while you work, and play while you play.

SPEECH OF RED JACKET, AN INDIAN CHIEF.

Brothers, listen to what we have to say: There was a time when our forefathers owned this great land; their seats extended from the rising to the setting sun; the Great Spirit had made it for the use of the Indians. He had created the buffalo, the deer, and other animals, for food. He had made the bear and the beaver; their skins served us for clothing. He had scattered them over the country, and taught us how to take them. He had caused the earth to produce corn for bread. All this he had done for his red children, because he loved them. If we had disputes about our hunting-grounds, they were generally settled without the shedding of much blood.

But an evil day came upon us: your forefathers crossed the great waters, and landed on this continent. Their numbers were small; they found us friends, and not enemies. They told us they had fled from their own country, through fear of wicked men, and had come here to enjoy their religion. They asked for a small seat: we took pity on them, and granted their request, and they sat down among us. We gave them corn and meat, and, in return, they gave us *poison.*

The white people having now found our country, tidings were sent back, and more came among us; yet we did not fear them. We took them to be friends — they called us *brothers;* and we believed them, and gave them a larger seat. At length their number so increased that they wanted more land; they wanted our whole country. Our eyes were now opened, and we became uneasy. Wars took place. Indians were hired to fight against Indians, and many of our people were destroyed. The white men also distributed *liquor* among us; and that has slain thousands.

You have now become a great people, and we have scarcely

a place left to spread our blankets. Having deprived us of our *country*, you would force upon us your *religion*. Brothers, we will wait a little, and, if we find the effect of your religion is to make people honest, and less disposed to cheat Indians, we will consider what you have said. And now may the Great Spirit protect you on your journey, and return you safe to your friends!

TRUE FRIENDSHIP.

If scandal or censure is raised 'gainst a friend,
Be the last to believe it, the first to defend;
Say to-morrow will come, and time will unfold,
That "one story 's good till another is told."

A friend 's like a ship when with music and song
The tide of good fortune still speeds him along;
But see him when tempest has made him a wreck,
And any mean billow may batter his deck!

So give me the heart that true sympathy shows,
And clings to a messmate whatever wind blows,
And says, when aspersion unanswered grows bold,
"Wait, — one story 's good till another is told."

CHARMING LITTLE VALLEY.

Charming little valley,
Smiling all so gayly,
Like an angel's brow;
Spreading out thy treasures,
Calling us to pleasures,
Innocent as thou:

Skies are bright above thee,
Peace and quiet love thee,
Tranquil little dell!
In thy fragrant bowers,
Twining wreaths of flowers,
Love and Friendship dwell.

May our spirits daily
Be like thee, sweet valley,
Tranquil and serene:
Emblem to us given
Of the vales of heaven,
Ever bright and green!

SPEAK NOT HARSHLY.

Speak not harshly! — much of care
Every human heart must bear;
Enough of shadows darkly lie
Veiled within the sunniest eye.
By thy childhood's gushing tears,
By thy griefs of after years,
By the anguish thou dost know,
Add not to another's woe.

Speak not harshly! — much of sin
Dwelleth every heart within;
In its closely-covered cells
Many a wayward passion dwells.
By thy many hours misspent,
By thy gifts to errors lent,
By the wrong thou didst not shun
By the good thou hast not done,
With a lenient spirit scan
The weakness of thy fellow-man.

THERE'S WORK ENOUGH TO DO.

The black-bird early leaves its rest,
  To meet the smiling morn,
And gather fragments for its nest
  From upland, wood, and lawn.
The busy bee, that wings its way
  'Mid sweets of varied hue,
And every flower, would seem to say,
  "There 's work enough to do."

The cowslip and the spreading vine,
  The daisy in the grass,
The snowdrop and the eglantine,
  Preach sermons as we pass.
The ant, within its cavern deep,
  Would bid us labor too,
And writes upon his tiny heap,
  "There 's work enough to do."

The planets, at their Maker's will,
  Move onward in their cars,

For Nature's will is never still —
  Progressive as the stars!
The leaves that flutter in the air,
  And Summer's breezes woo,
One solemn truth to man declare —
  "There 's work enough to do."

REPLY OF GRATTAN TO CORRY.

The right honorable gentleman has called me "an unimpeached traitor." I will not call him *villain*, because it would be unparliamentary, and he is a privy councilor. I will not call him *fool*, because he happens to be Chancellor of the Exchequer. But I say he is one who has abused the privilege of Parliament and freedom of debate to the uttering language, which, if spoken out of the house, I should only answer with a blow! I care not how high his situation, how low his character, how contemptible his speech; whether a privy councilor or a parasite, my answer would be a blow!

I have returned, not, as the right honorable member has said, to raise another storm; I have returned to discharge an honorable debt of gratitude to my country, that conferred a great reward for past services, which I am proud to say was not greater than my de-sert′; I have returned to protect that constitution of which I was the parent and the founder, from the assassination of such men as the honorable gentleman and his unworthy associates. They are corrupt; they are seditious; and, at this very moment, are in a conspiracy against their country!

I have returned to refute a libel, as false as it is malicious, given to the public under the appellation of a report of the committee of the Lords. Here I stand for impeachment or trial. I dare accusation. I defy the honorable gentleman.

I defy the government. I defy their whole phal'anx. Let them come forth! I tell the ministers I shall neither give quarter nor take it.

THE LIFE-BOAT.

QUICK! man the life-boat! See yon bark,
  That drives before the blast!
There 's a rock ahead, the fog is dark,
  And the storm comes thick and fast.
Can human power, in such an hour,
  Avert the doom that 's o'er her?
Her main-mast is gone, but she still drives on
  To the fatal reef before her.
    The life-boat! Man the life-boat!

Quick! man the life-boat! hark! the gun
  Booms through the vapory air;
And see! the signal-flags are on,
  And speak the ship's despair.
That forkëd flash, that pealing crash,
  Seemed from the wave to sweep her:
She 's on the rock, with a terrible shock —
  And the wail comes louder and deeper.
    The life-boat! Man the life-boat!

Quick! man the life-boat! See — the crew
  Gaze on their watery grave:
Already, some, a gallant few,
  Are battling with the wave;
And one there stands, and wrings his hands,
  As thoughts of home come o'er him;
For his wife and child, through the tempest wild,
  He sees on the heights before him.
    The life-boat! Man the life-boat!

Speed, speed the life-boat! Off she goes!
  And, as they pulled the oar,
From shore and ship a cheer arose
  That startled ship and shore.
Life-saving ark! yon fated bark
  Has human lives within her;
And dearer than gold is the wealth untold
  Thou 'lt save if thou canst win her.
    On, life-boat! Speed thee, life-boat!

Hurra! the life-boat dashes on,
  Though darkly the reef may frown;
The rock is there — the ship is gone
  Full twenty fathoms down.
But, cheered by hope, the seamen cope
  With the billows single-handed:
They are all in the boat! — hurra! they 're afloat! —
  And now they are safely landed,
    By the life-boat! Cheer the life-boat!

THE MOONLIGHT MARCH.

I SEE them on their winding way:
About their ranks the moonbeams play;
Their lofty deeds and daring high
Blend with the notes of victory.
And waving arms, and banners bright,
Are glancing in the mellow light:
They 're lost — and gone; the moon is past,
The wood's dark shade is o'er them cast;
And fainter, fainter, fainter still
The march is rising o'er the hill.

Again, again, the pealing drum,
The clashing horn — they come, they come!
Through rocky pass, o'er wooded steep,
In long and glittering files they sweep.
And nearer, nearer, yet more near,
Their softened chorus meets the ear.
Forth, forth, and meet them on their way!
The trampling hoofs brook no delay;
With thrilling fife, and pealing drum,
And clashing horn, they come, they come!

HEBER.

HAVE A PURPOSE.

If I were asked what attribute most commanded fortune, I should say "earnestness." The earnest man wins a way for himself, and earnestness and truth go together. Never affect to be other than you are — either richer or wiser. Never be ashamed to say, "I do not know." Men will then believe you when you say, "I do know."

Never be ashamed to say, whether as applied to time or money, "I can not afford it;" — "I can not afford to waste an hour in the idleness to which you invite me, — I can not afford the guinea you ask me to throw away." Once establish yourself and your mode of life as what they really are, and your foot is on solid ground, whether for the gradual step onward, or for the sudden spring over a precipice.

From these maxims let me deduce another, — learn to say "No" with decision; "Yes" with caution; — "No" with decision whenever it resists temptation; "Yes" with caution whenever it implies a promise. A promise once given is a bond inviolable. A man is already of consequence in the world when it is known that we can implicitly rely upon him.

I have frequently seen in life a person preferred to a long list of applicants, for some important charge which lifts him at once into station and fortune, merely because he has this reputation, that when he says he knows a thing, he knows it, and when he says he will do a thing, he will do it. Muse over these maxims; practice them! SIR E. B. LYTTON.

OUR CHURCHES AND SCHOOL-HOUSES.

ATTENTION to the wants of the intellect and of the soul, as manifested by the voluntary support of schools and colleges, of churches and benevolent institutions, is one of the most remarkable characteristics of the American people. It is not less strikingly exhibited in the new than in the older settlements of the country.

On the spot where the first trees of the forest are felled, near the log cabins of the pioneers, are to be seen rising together the church and the school-house. So has it been from the beginning, and God grant that it may ever thus continue!

"On other shores, above their mouldering towns,
In sullen pomp the tall cathedral frowns:
Simple and frail, our lowly temples throw
Their slender shadows on the paths below;
Scarce steals the wind, that sweeps the woodland tracks,
The larch's perfume from the settler's ax,
Ere, like a vision of the morning air,
His slight-framed steeple marks the house of prayer.

* * * * *

Yet Faith's pure hymn, beneath its shelter rude,
Breathes out as sweetly to the tangled wood,
As where the rays through blazing oriels pour
On marble shaft and tessellated floor."

WEBSTER.

THE ESQUIMAUX KAYAK.

The little skiff in which the Esquimaux (Es'ke-mo) hunts the seal is called a kay-ak'.

Over the briny wave I go,
In spite of the weather, in spite of the snow:
What cares the hardy Esquimaux?
In my little skiff, with paddle and lance,
I glide where the foaming billows dance:
And when the cautious seal I spy,
I poise my ready lance on high,
And then like lightning let it fly.

Round me the sea-birds dip and soar;
Like me they love the ocean's roar.
Sometimes a floating iceberg gleams
Over me with its melting streams.
Sometimes a rushing wave will fall
Down on my skiff, and cover it all.
But what care I for the waves' attack?
With my paddle I right my little kayak;
And then its freight I speedily trim,
And over the waters away I skim.

Ye who lead a delicate life,
Far from the ice and the billows' strife,
What would ye think to be with me
One hour upon this desolate sea? —
To glide where the young seals rise to breathe;
Where ridges of foam about them wreathe;
To stand on the ice where the walrus plays;
Or, hungry and savage, the white bear strays.
O! how would ye fancy sport like this?
Yet to me, ye men of the city, 't is bliss!

THE FRENCHMAN'S LESSON IN ENGLISH.

Frenchman. Ha, my friend! I have met one very strange word in my lesson. Vat you call c-h-o-u-g-h, eh?

Tutor. Chuff. A chough is a bird of the crow family.

Fr. Tres bien, very well; c-h-o-u-g-h is chuff; and snuff you spell s-n-o-u-g-h, eh?

Tu. O, no, no! snuff is spelled s-n-u-f-f. In fact, our words in *ough* are a little irregular.

Fr. Ah! Very good! 'T is beautiful language! — C-h-o-u-g-h is chuff. I will remember; and of course c-o-u-g-h is kuff; I have one very bad kuff, eh?

Tu. No, that is wrong: we say kauff, not kuff.

Fr. Kauff, eh? Chuff and kauff. Ver' well; but, pardonnez moi, pardon me, how you call d-o-u-g-h — duff, eh? Is it duff?

Tu. No, not duff.

Fr. Not duff? Ah, oui; I understand — it is dauff, ha?

Tu. No; d-o-u-g-h spells doe.

Fr. Doe! It is ver' fine! — wonderful language! it is doe! Eh bien! Then t-o-u-g-h is toe, eh? My beef-steak is toe!

Tu. O, no, no! You should say tuff.

Fr. Tuff? O, ver' well! We will find it out bientôt, by and by. The thing the farmer uses — how call you him, p-l-o-u-g-h, — pluff, is it? Ha, you smile; I am wrong, I see; then it must be plauff. No? Then it is ploe, like doe? Beautiful language! Ploe!

Tu. You are still wrong, my friend; it is plow.

Fr. O, ver' well. Plow! I shall understand ver' soon. Plow, doe, kauff, chuff! I vill try to recollect. But here is one word, h-o-u-g-h, which means the joint of the leg of one beast. Do you call it huff?

Tu. No.

Fr. Hauff?

Tu. No.

Fr. Hoe?

Tu. No.

Fr. How?

Tu. No.

Fr. Huff?

Tu. No.

Fr. O, the beautiful language! Tell me what, then, is h-o-u-g-h?

Tu. We pronounce the word hŏk.

Fr. Hok! O, but that is delightful! Ver' beautiful language! One more word I have: r-o-u-g-h — is it rok? Do you call General Taylor, Rok and Ready? No? Is it then Row and Ready, or Roe and Ready? No? Is it then Rauf and Ready?

Tu. No, no! R-o-u-g-h spells ruff.

Fr. It is ruff, is it? Let me not forget. And b-o-u-g-h is buff, eh? The buff of a tree!

Tu. O, no! B-o-u-g-h is bow.

Fr. Ah! 't is ver' simple! Wonderful language! But I

have had — what you call e-n-o-u-g-h, ha? vat you call him? Enok, or enow, or enoe?

Tu. We say enuff.

Fr. O! then I say enuff, too. I have had quite enuff for one lesson! Bon jour, monsieur!

A MOTHER'S GIFT.

Remember, love, who gave thee this,
  When other days shall come, —
When she who had thine earliest kiss
  Sleeps in her narrow home.
Remember, 't was a mother gave
The gift to one she 'd die to save!

That mother sought a pledge of love,
  The holiest for her son;
And from the gifts of God above
  She chose a goodly one: —
She chose for her belovëd boy
The source of light, and life, and joy.

And bǎde him keep the gift, that when
  The parting hour should come,
They might have hope to meet again,
  In an eternal home.
She said his faith in this would be
Sweet incense to her memory.

And should the scoffer, in his pride.
  Laugh that fond faith to scorn,
And bid him cast the pledge aside,
  That he from youth had bōrne,
She bade him pause, and ask his breast
If she, or he, had loved him best.

A parent's blessing on her son
  Goes with this holy thing;
The love that would retain the one
  Must to the other cling.
Remember — 't is no idle toy —
A mother's gift — remember, boy!

KENNEDY.

CORN-FIELDS.

When on the breath of autumn's breeze,
  From pastures dry and brown,
Goes floating, like an idle thought,
  The fair, white thistle-down, —
O, then what joy to walk at will
Upon the golden harvest-hill!

What joy in dreamy ease to lie
  Amid a field new-shōrn,
And see all round, on sunlit slopes,
  The piled-up shocks of corn,
And send the fancy wandering o'er
All pleasant harvest-fields of yore!

I feel the day; I see the field;
  The quivering of the leaves;
And good old Jacob and his house
  Binding the yellow sheaves!
And at this very hour I seem
To be with Joseph in his dream!

I see the fields of Bethlehem,
  And reapers many a one
Bending unto their sickle's stroke,
  And Boäz looking on;

And Ruth, the Moäbitess fair,
Among the gleaners stooping there!

Again, I see a little child,
His mother's sole delight;
God's living gift of love unto
The kind, good Shunamite;
To mortal pangs I see him yield,
And the lad bear him from the field.

The sun-bathed quiet of the hills,
The fields of Galilee,
That eighteen hundred years ago
Were full of corn, I see;
And the dear Saviour take his way
'Mid ripe ears on the Sabbath day.

O, golden fields of bending corn,
How beautiful they seem!
The reaper-folk, the piled-up sheaves,
To me are like a dream;
The sunshine and the very air
Seem of old time, and take me there!

MARY HOWITT.

WHAT IS PROPERTY?

YONDER stands an old tree which I call *mine*. Other generations before me have dwelt under its shade, and called it *theirs;* and other generations after me will do the same. And yet I call the tree mine. A bird has built a nest on one of its highest branches, but I can not reach it, and yet I call the tree mine.

Mine! There is scarcely any thing which I call mine which will not last much longer in this world than I shall:

there is not a single button of my jacket that is not destined to survive me many years.

What a strange thing is this *property* of which men are so envious! When I had *nothing of my own*, I had forests and meadows, and the sea, and the sky with all its stars!

I remember an old wood near to the house in which I was born. What days have I passed under its thick shade, in its green alleys! What violets have I gathered in it in the month of April, and what lilies of the valley in the month of May! What strawberries, blackberries, and nuts, I have eaten in it! What butterflies I have chased there! What nests I have discovered! What sweet per′fumes * have I inhaled! What verses have I there made! How often have I gone thither at the close of day, to see the glorious sun set, coloring with red and gold the white trunks of the birch-trees around me!

This wood was not *mine;* it belonged to an old bed-ridden miser, who had, perhaps, never been in it in his life — and yet *it belonged to him.* FROM THE FRENCH OF KARR.

ON EARLY RISING.

Falsely luxurious, will not man awake,
And, springing from the bed of sloth, enjoy
The cool, the fragrant, and the silent hour,
To meditation due, and sacred song? —
Wildered and tossing through distempered dreams, —
Who would in such a gloomy state remain
Longer than nature craves, when every Muse
And every blooming pleasure wait without
To bless the wildly-devious morning walk?

THOMSON.

* *Perfume,* when a noun, has the accent on the first syllable; when a verb, on the last.

THE BOBOLINK AND THE SPORTSMAN. — A Fable.

A Bobolink, whose lucky lot
It was to dodge a sportsman's shot,
Perched on a hemlock-bough, began
To taunt the disappointed man: —

"Click! bang! Put in more powder, Mister!
Tall shooting that! Call in your sister!
Shoot with a shovel, you'd do better!
Ha! Rip-si-da'dy! I'm your debtor!
Chick-a-dee-dee! Don't pine in sorrow!
You could n't do it. Call to-morrow!
You'll always find me in. Tip-wheet!
You're a great fool! Hip! Zip! Bang! Skeet!
Lick-a-tee-split! No, no! You can't! —
My best remembrance to your aunt!
Chick-a-dee-dee! Tip-wheet! I never
Felt better! Bobolinks for ever!
You thought you had me fast asleep. —
Excuse my laughing: you look cheap.
Come, try again; don't quit your gaming;
I feel so safe when you are aiming!"

The sportsman angry grew: another
Drew near, and thus addressed his brother:
"When your attempts to injure fail,
Complain not if your victim rail."

THE THUNDER-SHOWER.

SINCE morning the heavens have been concealed by thick clouds; the air is heavy, and respiration difficult. The birds have ceased to sing; the bees will not go beyond the garden-walls; the flowers, half-faded, seem to languish on their stalks; swallows fly about, skimming the earth.

A flash of lightning gleams from a black cloud, and is followed by a heavy, distant sound. The flashes soon become more frequent, the peals of thunder nearer; then the clouds burst,* and the rain falls in torrents!

And then the freshened air deliciously dilates the lungs; the honeysuckles spread abroad their sweetest per'fumes; the earth itself throws up a delightful odor; the rain has ceased, and the sun converts into fiery diamonds the drops suspended from the leaves of the trees. Pardon me, beautiful drops of rain, for comparing you to diamonds!

The birds sing, the flowers resume their splendor, and lift up their heads. Every thing is revived, fresh, smiling, happy!

SPEECH OF A POCOMTUCK INDIAN.

WHITE man, there is eternal war between me and thee. I quit not the land of my fathers, but with my life. Whither shall I fly? Shall I wander to the west? — The fierce Mohawk, the man-eater, is my foe. Shall I fly to the east? — The

* The *ur* in *burst* and the *ir* in *first* have the sound of *er* in *her*.

great water is before me. No, stranger: here I have lived, and here will I die; and, if here thou abidest, there is eternal war between me and thee. Thou hast taught me thy arts of destruction; for that alone I thank thee. And now take heed to thy steps: the red man is thy foe. When thou goest forth by day, my bullet shall whistle by thee; when thou liest down at night, my knife shall be at thy throat. The noonday sun shall not discover thy enemy, and the darkness of midnight shall not protect thy rest. Thou shalt plant in terror, and I will reap in blood; thou shalt sow the earth with corn, and I will strew it with ashes; thou shalt go forth with the sickle, and I will follow after with the scalping-knife; thou shalt build, and I will burn, till the white man or the Indian shall cease from the land! EVERETT.

THE WOLF AND THE KID. — A FABLE.

COWARDS most insolent appear
When sure that they have naught to fear.

A Kid, who felt secure and bold,
High walled within his master's fold,
Seeing a Wolf beneath him go,
Cried out, "Thief! villain! booby! Ho!
Come up here, and I 'll put you through! —
You dare not? What, a coward too?
Look here, old fellow! how 's your mother?
Are you as handsome as your brother?
Before you go, unless you 'd grieve me,
Don't fail a lock of hair to leave me.
You sneaking rascal, base and cruel,
Come here, I 'll serve you out your gruel!
You would n't like me for your dinner?
O, no! you old bloodthirsty sinner!

Only come here, and you shall find
Some grub not wholly to your mind!
Of you, and twenty like you, I
Am not afraid. Come on and try! —
But here 's my master, with his rifle:
Be off, you scamp! your time you trifle."

The Wolf looked up and shook his head,
And, smiling grimly, merely said,
"My dear, rail on! I care not how —
For 't is the wall that speaks, not thou."

GREAT RESULTS FROM SMALL CAUSES.

From trifling causes what mighty effects may flow! Events which seemed insignificant at the moment, have been the germ of the most momentous consequences.

A spectacle-maker's boy was one day amusing himself in his father's shop by holding two glasses between his finger and thumb. By varying their distance, the weathercock of the church-spire opposite to him seemed larger and nearer, and turned upside down. He showed it to his father; it excited his wonder, and led to experiments which resulted in that astonishing instrument, the telescope, as invented by Gal-i-le′o, and perfected by Herschel.

On the same optical principles was constructed the microscope, by which we perceive that a drop of stagnant water is a world teeming with inhabitants.

By the telescope, the experimental philosopher measures the ponderous globes, that the Omnipotent Hand has ranged in majestic order through the skies; by the microscope, he sees that the same hand has rounded and polished five thousand minute transparent globes in the eye of a fly. Yet all these discoveries of modern science, exhibiting the intelligence, dominion, and agency of God, we owe to the transient amusement of a child!

SAUL, BEFORE HIS LAST BATTLE.

WARRIORS and chiefs! should the shaft or the sword
Pierce me in leading the hosts of the Lord,
Heed not the corse, though a king's, in your path;
Bury your steel in the bosom of Gath!

Thou who art bearing my buckler and bow,
Should the soldiers of Saul look away from the foe,
Stretch me that moment in blood at thy feet!
Mine be the doom which they dared not to meet!

Farewell to others, but never we part,
Heir to my royalty, son of my heart!
Bright is the diadem, boundless the sway,
Or kingly the death, which awaits us to-day.

BYRON.

COMMON BOUNTIES.

"Is it not a beautiful flower?" I asked, plucking a violet, and offering it to my friend. — "Yes, but then it is so common!" said he. — "And why should we prize its beauty the less on that account?"

Thanks, O Lord, for all that thou hast created *common!* Thanks for the blue heavens, the sun, the stars, murmuring waters, and the shade of embowering oaks! Thanks for the corn-flowers of the fields and the gilly-flowers* of the walls! Thanks for the songs of the robin, and the hymns of the

* Pronounced *jilly-flower*. The word is said to be corrupted from *July-flower*.

nightingale! Thanks for the per′fumes of the air, and the sighing of the winds among the trees! Thanks for the magnificent clouds gilded by the sun at its setting and rising! Thanks for love, the most common sentiment of all! Thanks for all the beautiful things which Thy stupendous bounty has made *common!*

EXECUTION OF ANDREW HOFER.

ANDREW HOFER, a gallant leader of the Tyrolese, was shot by his country's oppressors, February 20th, 1810. — In pronouncing *Tyrol,* put the accent on the last syllable.

AT Mantua, in chains, the gallant Hofer lay;
In Mantua, to death, the foe led him away;
Right bravely had he striven, in arms, to make a stand
For freedom and Ty-rol′, his own fair mountain land.

His hands behind him clasped, with firm and measured pace,
Marched Andrew Hofer on: he feared not death to face;
"Ty-rol′, I hoped to see your sons and daughters free!
Farewell, my mountain land! a last farewell!" said he

The drummer's hand refused to beat the funeral march
While Andrew Hofer passed the portal's gloomy arch:
He on the bastion stood, the shackles on his arm,
But proudly and erect, as if he feared no harm.

They băde him then kneel down: said he, "That will I not!
Here standing will I die, as I *have* stood and fought!
No tyrant's power shall claim from me the bended knee;
I'll die as I have lived — for thee, Ty-rol′, for thee!"

A grenadier then took the bandage from his hand,
While Hofer breathed a prayer, his last on earthly land:
"Aim well, my lads!" said he: — the soldiers aimed and fired.
"For thee, Ty-rol′, I die!" said Hofer — and expired.

THE STEP-LADDER. — A FABLE.

ONCE on a time, a sparrow, while on the look-out for something to eat, caught a big blue-bottle fly on a branch of a weeping-willow. "O! let me go, there's a good fellow," cried the fly. — "No," said the murderer, "not at all! for I am big, and you are small."

While the sparrow was swallowing the poor fly, a sparrow-hawk pounced on the bird, and clutched him in his talons. "O! let me go! What have I done? Be merciful!" cried the sparrow. — "No," said the murderer, "not at all! for I am big, and you are small."

An eagle spied the sport, and thought he would drop in to have a bit of dinner: so he seized the sparrow-hawk by the throat. "O, please your majesty, let me go!" cried the sparrow-hawk; "have mercy on a worthless sinner." — "Pooh!" said the murderer; "not at all! for I am big, and you are small."

While the eagle was picking the sparrow-hawk's bones, an archer came along with his bow and arrow, and, spying the eagle, sent an arrow to his heart. "Ah me! how cruel!" exclaimed the eagle.—"Nonsense!" quoth the archer; "not at all! for I am big, and you are small!"

ON INAUGURATING THE STATUE OF WARREN,

ON BUNKER HILL, JUNE 17TH, 1857.

MY friends, let the recollections of a common danger and a common glory bring with them the strengthened love of a common country. It may be doubted whether the most brilliant success on Bunker Hill could have done as much to bind the colonies together as the noble, though in its immediate results unavailing, resistance; the profuse, though at the time unprofitable, outpouring of human blood.

A great revolution must be inaugurated with a great sacrifice, and all the loftier passions are ennobled by the purification of sorrow; nor is it certain that Warren, had he assumed the command and driven the enemy back to his boats, would have done as much to kindle a chastised and resolute enthusiasm throughout the country, and unite the colonies in the impending struggle, as when he shouldered his musket and fell in the ranks.

And, O! my friends, let the lesson of fraternal affection which he taught us in his death be repeated in the persuasive silence of those stony lips! In his own heart-stirring language, let "the voice of our fathers' blood cry to us from the ground;" and, upon this sacred day, and on this immortal hill, let it proclaim a truce to sectional alienation and party strife.

Wherever else the elements of discord may rage, let the billows sink down, and the storm be hushed, like yonder placid waves, at the foot of Bunker Hill! Here let the kindly feelings that animated our fathers revive in the bosoms of their sons, assured that — should "malice domestic or foreign levy" invade us — if living champions should fail, that monumental cheek would burn with the glow of patriotism, that marble sword would leap from its scabbard, and the heaving sods of Bunker Hill give up their sheeted regiments to the defence of the Union! EVERETT.

THE HELP OF THE HUMBLE.

SMALL service is true service while it lasts;
Of friends, however humble, scorn not one:
The daisy, by the shadow that it casts,
Protects the lingering dew-drop from the sun.

WORDSWORTH.

THE PRUSSIAN GENERAL ON THE RHINE.

'T WAS on the Rhine the armies lay : —
To France or not? Is 't yea or nay?
They pondered long, and pondered well;
At length old Blucher broke the spell :
" Bring here the map to me!
The road to France is straight and free : —
Where is the foe?" — "The foe? Why, here!"—
"We 'll beat him. Forward! Never fear!
Say, where lies Paris?" — "Paris? — here!"
"We 'll take it. Forward! Never fear!
So throw a bridge across the Rhine :
Methinks the Frenchman's sparkling wine
Will taste the best where grows the vine!"

FROM THE GERMAN OF KOPISCH.

THE BETTER LAND.

I HEAR thee speak of the better land :
Thou call'st its children a happy band;
Mother, O, where is that radiant shore—
Shall we not seek it, and weep no more?
Is it where the flower of the orange blows,
And the fire-flies dance through the myrtle boughs?
"Not there, not there, my child."

Is it where the feathery palm-trees rise,
And the date grows ripe under sunny skies,
Or 'mid the green islands of glittering seas,
Where fragrant forests perfume the breeze,
And strange bright birds on their starry wings
Bear the rich hues of all glorious things?
"Not there, not there, my child."

Is it far away in some region old,
Where the rivers wander o'er sands of gold, —
Where the burning rays of the ruby shine,
And the diamond lights up the secret mine,
And the pearl gleams forth from the coral strand, —
Is it there, sweet mother, that better land?
  "Not there, not there, my child.

"Eye hath not seen it, my gentle boy!
Ear hath not heard its deep songs of joy,
Dreams can not picture a world so fair, —
Sorrow and death may not enter there;
Time doth not breathe on its fadeless bloom,
For beyond the clouds, and beyond the tomb,
  It is there, it is there, my child!"

MRS. HEMANS.

www.ingramcontent.com/pod-product-compliance
Lightning Source LLC
LaVergne TN
LVHW021404110826
845150LV00007B/1782

* 9 7 8 1 4 2 5 5 1 2 6 4 4 *